A Guide for Board Chairs of Jesuit Colleges and Universities

Cover art by Holly Schapker. "Ignatius," *Ad Sum* Collection.

Contents

Dear Board Chair,

Peace!

On behalf of the Association of Jesuit Colleges and Universities (AJCU), I want to thank you for your dedicated service as the chair of your Jesuit institution's Board of Trustees. The entire network of AJCU colleges and universities in North America and internationally is better for the time, thought, and creative leadership that you exercise. This responsibility for governance of a Jesuit university is no small commitment. Whether you are an incoming chair or a veteran in the work, you will surely experience both the joys and the challenges of the position. Please know that the Society of Jesus, AJCU, and your own school are deeply indebted to you for your generous gifts of time and talent.

Leadership of your Board is part of the larger religious enterprise of Jesuit education with its global reach and 500-year tradition of educating young people to become morally sensitive, courageous leaders of their communities. Our aim in every Jesuit college and university is to prepare students for the creation of a more just, loving, and sustainable world. Trustees are a vital part of that effort.

This AJCU *Guide for Board Chairs* plays a small but important part in preparing you for your role as chair. It is the product of many contributors, each of whom has long and deep experience with Boards in Jesuit higher education. This first edition will doubtless undergo changes in the future, and we welcome your suggestions. You may choose to read it cover to cover or keep it close at hand as a reference book. You may also wish to share selected chapters or the entire text with your Executive Committee or Board, a task made easier by the availability of an e-book version online.

By strengthening your Board's mission competency and equipping trustees to play their critical role in the great enterprise of Jesuit higher education, you are helping your entire institution to become a well-governed, mission-led, discerning community. In short, you are making our Catholic, Jesuit mission credible and effective.

With appreciation and a commitment to support you as you lead your Board,

Rev. Michael J. Garanzini, S.J.
President

Introduction

History and Context

Ignatius of Loyola (1491-1556) did not intend to found a religious order when he and a group of fellow students at the University of Paris bound themselves together with simple religious vows. Their original goal was merely to help people in body and soul, especially by means of preaching and spiritual accompaniment, under the rubric of the Spiritual Exercises that Ignatius had developed prior to his arrival in Paris. By 1540, that group of seven had received permission from Pope Paul III to become an order within the Catholic Church. The new community grew quickly, so houses of formation were soon established for the education of young Jesuits. By 1548, in Messina, Sicily, the first school for lay students was opened at the request of parents who wanted the same humanistic education that Jesuits were offering to their members to be available to all young men, in preparation for adult life as committed lay Catholics.

The Jesuits learned that schools were excellent platforms, not only for the formation of youth, but also to engage their parents and, indeed, whole towns and cities. In the decades and centuries that followed, the Jesuits and their lay companions built primary, secondary, and tertiary schools across Europe and around the world. Today, there are about 3,700 such schools educating some

2.5 million students and supporting alumni networks many times that size.

Fifty years ago in American Jesuit higher education, the universities were owned by the Jesuits and their governance was in the hands of local rectors and superiors, regional provincials, and their consultors (including an official board of advisors for provincials and superiors of Jesuit communities). Provincials, in turn, answered — as they continue to do — to the general superior in Rome. Beginning in the 1960s and early 1970s, lay Boards of trustees were inaugurated in order to professionalize governance and strengthen academic freedom. As the social, legal, and economic frameworks of Jesuit universities became far more complex throughout the 1970s, the schools adopted structures and professional standards akin to their nonsectarian peers. Yet, even amid these changes, the mission and élan of Jesuit colleges and universities perdures.

Whether you visit a Jesuit school in Nairobi, Mexico City, Philadelphia, Manila, or Berlin, you will find that — while they are anchored firmly in their local cultures, economies, and environments — there is a strong family resemblance among them. These sister schools reflect diverse contexts, and their pedagogy and curricula can be quite specialized. Yet they are built upon the same premise: to help students experience the grace of God and thereby find their true vocation in life; and to serve, live, and lead *ad maiorem Dei gloriam*, the Jesuit motto meaning "for the greater glory of God."

The Board's Role in Mission Governance

Board chairs can rest assured that the institutions entrusted to their care are heirs to this history and respected parts of the worldwide Jesuit community of ministries. The Society of Jesus is ready to consult, collaborate, evaluate, and endorse your school. To that end, the ***AJCU and the Society provide resources, committed colleagues, and programs to help you and your fellow trustees govern in a mission-centric way.*** There are online and in-person opportunities for chairs to become active learners and contributing thinkers in this network.

The word "network" is an important one. The AJCU in North America consists of 28 member schools in the U.S. and Belize, along with four associate member schools in Canada and Australia. Similarly, the International Association of Jesuit Universities (IAJU), of which AJCU is a part, represents nearly 200 Jesuit higher education institutions around the world. These are voluntary networks, not centrally governed systems, and they offer rich opportunities for collaboration across schools and countries. Your institution benefits from actively engaging with both.

That being said, ***trustees of AJCU colleges and universities have full and final authority to govern their***

school according to its bylaws and in fulfillment of its Catholic and Jesuit mission and identity. It is their responsibility to assure that the school is and remains a Jesuit work, and as such, a Catholic institution. For a brief history of the development of independent Jesuit university Boards, see the fall 2023 edition of *In Fides* (formerly titled *In Trust*), AJCU's biannual, online magazine for trustees, listed at the end of this chapter.

Board Formation

It is important for chairs to know a fair amount about the history and traditions of their college or university. Who were the Jesuit and lay scientists and poets, scholars and jurists, founders and public servants who taught at, or graduated from, their school? What role has athletics or the arts played in bringing alumni and friends back to campus? What common experiences and narratives have united the university community?

By extension, getting to know the school's mission, stories, and culture is essential work for trustees. Mission, vision, and values statements are descriptive and aspirational documents, but they are also normative, which is to say they shape the plans, principles, and priorities that undergird even the most difficult choices each school will make. While specific decisions of the Board may not be universally popular, they will be intelligible and defensible if they are based upon your school's articulation of its

Catholic identity and Jesuit mission. It is within the chair's scope of leadership to serve as a mission guide, making connections between the Board's business and the mission considerations that inform governance.

How to live the mission should never be a topic relegated to a few trustees. Rather, chairs can help all trustees grow in their own mission capacity and commitment.

The chair — well advised by the chief mission officer and president — serves as a de facto guide for trustee formation. If someone is "too busy" for such formation, then they are too busy to serve as a trustee of a Jesuit work. Free them up to pursue matters that are more important to them.

Practically speaking, some Boards are structured in such a way that new trustees spend their first few years on the Catholic Identity and Jesuit Mission Committee. Others devote annual retreats to mission formation or consistently include "Mission Moments" or an Ignatian Examen in their meetings. In every committee and agenda of the Board, trustees must see and exercise the "business" of running a Jesuit university through the lens of its mission.

Board chairs have much to learn from gathering with other mission leaders. AJCU and the Jesuit Conference of Canada and the United States (JCCU) sponsor a triennial meeting for all Board chairs, presidents, and provincials, at which the current reality and future of Jesuit higher education are discussed. All three constituencies report that these meetings are fundamental to advancing our shared project and for mutual support.

Resources for trustee mission formation are also available through AJCU's Trustee Forum, a deep-dive event for trustees to explore mission governance and learn from their peers: https://tinyurl.com/AJCUTrusteeForum.

Recommended Reading

Collins, D. (2023). *The Jesuits in the United States: A concise history*. Georgetown University Press.

Garanzini, M.J. (2023 Fall). The responsibilities of trustees at Jesuit institutions: A brief history. *In Fides. (1),* 7-15. https://tinyurl.com/InFidesFall2023

O'Malley, J. W. (2017). *The Jesuits: A history from Ignatius to the present*. Rowman and Littlefield Publishers.

Rizzi, M. T. (2022). *Jesuit colleges and universities in the United States: A history*. Catholic University of America Press.

Chapter 1
Leadership and Governance

Supporting and Guiding the President

As chief executive officer, the president is assisted by the chief academic officer or provost, chief financial officer, general counsel, chief mission officer, and vice presidents for all other core functions. While the chief mission officer oversees the advancement of the mission at the institution, ***the president is the principal mission officer at a Jesuit institution, uniquely charged with the essential role of embodying the core values of the school and assuring that they are universally applied.*** The Board chair, then, works to endorse and support the president as mission leader. In Jesuit terms, the president is the "director of the work," a title that is affirmed by the provincial at the inauguration of all new presidents.

It is essential that the Board chair and university president work as a cohesive team, with regular — normally weekly — check-ins. Many of the president's daily activities are too mundane or detailed to be shared, but there will be a steady stream of important decisions to be made, crises to be faced, and long-term strategies to be considered. These should be the subjects of ongoing discussion between the president and the chair. Having a sense of the president's workload can lead to discussions on how the chair and the Board might support and counsel the president in carrying out responsibilities with diverse communities and community leaders.

Others lay claim to the president's time as well. Lay presidents may have families and Jesuit presidents report to a religious superior. Each will have commitments to balance and will relate to students, faculty, and staff in ways consistent with their vocation. A deft chair will affirm and support the president's vocation, extending to the president the same *cura personalis* (meaning "care for the individual person") that the school provides for students, faculty, and staff.

Board chairs have unique opportunities to serve as counselors, confidants, trusted advisors, and sounding boards for presidents.

Friendship is a plus, but objectivity, respect, and charity are required. Regular communication between the chair and president is essential. Being a college or university president these days is a very complex and stressful job with more critics than fans. The instantaneous effects of social media alone put immense pressure on presidents to respond quickly to concerns, lest the institution's reputation suffer.

To insert an element of calm and collegiality, consider scheduling in-person meetings with the president during the first few years of your partnership. Virtual meetings are a good way to maintain a relationship but much less helpful in trying to forge one. Regularly inquire, “How are you doing?” and “How are things going?” Know that presidents typically appreciate a supportive phone call or text message, particularly when facing a challenge. They also value messages of congratulations and knowing that you are thinking of them.

The relationship between a chair and president is a privileged one. Discretion and trust are key when the president is seeking the chair’s help in understanding and dealing with trustees who may be overstepping boundaries or becoming hypercritical. Keeping confidences with and for the president does not mean failing to report matters that may be unethical or illegal. However, confidentiality in above-board matters is necessary to afford the president the requisite time and space to come to a considered decision in a complex situation.

Since neither the chair nor any of the trustees supervises the vice presidents — even in the context of Board committees — the president needs to know when a trustee is interacting with a vice president. The Board supervises one employee only: the president. Good communication between senior leadership and trustees is important, and effective trustees will have good working relationships with vice presidents and deans. However, interactions should always take place with the knowledge of the president.

Core Duties of a Board

The Association of Governing Boards of Universities and Colleges (AGB) is a valuable resource and a treasure trove of information for college and university trustees across the country. Each school's AGB membership provides access to materials, programs, and consultations that can greatly benefit their Board's work and functioning. The chair should be familiar with the organization's many offerings and make use of them whenever possible. Learn more at agb.org.

1. Selecting a new president

One of the most important tasks of any college or university Board arises when it becomes necessary to select a new president. Chapter 10 of this *Guide* provides added insight on the presidential search process, but a few headlines are important to mention here:

- The position description and search process used in the previous presidential hire provide a good starting place, but both will need to be recast, based on the Board's best understanding of the current and near future needs of the institution and the current market for talented, available leaders.
- Regional and national Jesuit leaders will be valuable consultants. The faculty and staff of the institution will bring helpful insights. Students and alumni will want to

share their opinions. In the end, however, the responsibility for hiring the next president rests fully and finally with the Board.

- The chair will be a key player in the transition and on-boarding of a new president. If necessary, the Board should extend the chair's term to cover the first year of the new president's service.
- Keep in mind that interviews between finalists and university leaders are a two-way process: Boards will want their first-choice candidate to make the school their top pick as well. A well-functioning Board is an important selling point for desirable presidential candidates.

2. Strategic planning for the future of the institution

The president, working with a full complement of university leadership and consulting a wide range of constituencies, will regularly develop strategic and tactical plans for the institution. This planning includes, but is not exclusive to, forecasting and driving marketing/recruitment/enrollment, physical facilities, technology infrastructure and data security, new or revised academic programs, fundraising campaigns, and other vital initiatives. It is not the Board's task to participate in the elaboration of any of these plans but, rather, to ask good questions along the way about quality assurance, projected cost, return on investment, and especially mission alignment. As fully formed plans are brought before the Board for approval with the consent of appropriate Board committees, the Board will approve these plans and oversee their implementation, monitoring milestones and assuring quality in the months and years to come. Further discussion on the Board's role in strategic planning is treated in Chapter 5 of this *Guide.*

3. Fiduciary responsibility

The Board owns and is responsible for the institution. The chair assures that the Board exercises its fiduciary responsibilities, including supervision of the management of monies and properties, the fulfillment of contractual obligations, and the proper defense of the institution from legal complaints. Other fiduciary responsibilities of the Board include:

- Receiving from the administration and approving the annual operating budget, the acquisition of property, and any new debt covenants (above a reasonable threshold)
- Approving the annual capital budget and special capital projects
- Assuring competent oversight of the endowment, monitoring its performance, seeing that ethical investment policies are followed, and ensuring that endowment pay-outs support the purposes stipulated by the original benefactors or intervening court orders
- Delegating appropriate representatives of the Board to meet with external auditors, accepting the annual external audit, and presenting this to the Board for notification

4. Developing resources for the advancement of the institution

Philanthropy, along with federal and state grants, plays an essential role in the financing of all Jesuit institutions, especially as the national landscape of external funding is changing at a rapid pace. Net tuition revenue typically does not cover annual operating costs. Current-use gifts and grants, plus endowment distributions, close the gap. Jesuit schools often need the help of benefactors to renew, replace, and expand physical facilities, whether they be student housing, academic buildings, athletic facilities, or flexible programming spaces. Boards should seek to expand their endowments so that, over time, their schools remain affordable for students and families at all income levels.

The Board approves and supports each comprehensive campaign, with the chair serving as a visible and credible advocate for its goals. At the time of their election, each trustee should have agreed to (a) make the college or university their first, second, or third most important philanthropic commitment, (b) make annual gifts exceeding a specified threshold, and (c) make a stretch gift during a campaign. The Board chair will be instrumental in reminding trustees of these agreements, instilling a sense of urgency, and setting an example as an ambassador of the institution.

5. Approvals of academic programs

Boards usually approve the launching and closing of degree programs. Processes are in place for assessing the viability and appropriateness of a new degree program. Criteria for ceasing to operate a program are also Board-approved. In a similar vein, approving revisions to the core curriculum are often the duty of the Board, a policy recommended by accrediting agencies. This is a key area of faculty engagement and part of the shared governance processes of universities. See Chapter 6 for more on the Board's participation in shared governance.

Responsibilities Outside the Board's Scope

Just as it is important to describe the Board's duties, so, too, it is important to note what the Board is *not* charged to do. The Board does not manage the university. Well-meaning Boards can sometimes exceed their scope, which sows general confusion and can demoralize the administration. Overreach is especially tempting in times of financial crisis or external pressure. As appealing as it may be for trustees to participate in the hiring of the next head basketball coach, the dean of the business school, or even an endowed chair established by a trustee's family, the Board as a whole and each of its members have delegated the running of the university to the administration. As the saying goes, "Noses in, fingers out."

The vice presidents will have established, in consultation with the trustee chairs of the appropriate Board committees, strategic and tactical goals with metrics and milestones. ***Trustees should be content with high-level analysis and must resist the urge to wander into the weeds.*** If trustees are concerned that a vice president is failing to meet the established goals, this is a matter for the Board to take up with the president. It would be highly unusual, even after due process, for the Board to overturn an operational decision made by the president.

The Public-Facing Role of Trustees

Trustees should think of themselves as public advocates or ambassadors for the institution. Because of their intimate knowledge of the university, they are well placed to speak about its strengths, the benefits of matriculating to the school, and the institution's contributions to the city and country. They should be able to cite statistics or point to examples that identify the institution's accomplishments.

Occasionally, however, being ambassadors can put trustees in embarrassing situations. Someone seeking employment at the school may importune a trustee to write a letter of support or intervene more overtly. A good response to this sort of request is, "We trustees have delegated all operating decisions to the school's leadership." A family may contact a trustee with the request that the trustee help overturn a negative admissions decision or direct an increase in a financial aid offer. Trustees can respond with, "I will relay your concern, but there are professionals in the admissions and financial aid offices who, I hope, have all of the pertinent, even confidential, information and who understand these matters in depth."

Since institutions of higher education are very complex politically, trustees in general, and the Board chair in particular, should portray themselves as above the political squabbles of the moment. A rule of thumb is to seek legal counsel's input whenever needed for matters involving this important group. Favors, conflicts of interest, conditions placed on gifts, and bending institutional policy on admissions of children, spouses, relatives, or friends can be delicate and present an awkward situation for the president. Trustee interventions in disciplinary matters involving students, faculty, and staff can be downright harmful to the institution. Whether it is a faculty tenure denial, a student disciplinary matter, or a staff evaluation appeal, trustees should avoid being dragged into debates. Complainants have further recourse through internal appeals or external legal pursuits. Trustees need not go there.

In sum, the administrative leadership of the college or university is charged with — and is professionally qualified to fulfill — the strategic directions approved by the Board. The president's team oversees and manages day-to-day operations and administrative tasks. Just as the Board of Trustees renews itself as current members term out or resign, so too does the administration renew itself and the corpus of faculty and staff. Trustees can help with blue sky brainstorming, but senior management develops and deploys academic programs aligned with the school's mission, as articulated in the strategic plan.

Through the practice of shared governance, administration and faculty agree which deliberative processes will receive input and serious consideration regarding matters that affect the life of faculty and their pedagogical and scholarly duties. Most conversations regarding institutional policies benefit by consultation. These structures of shared governance are specified in each school's faculty handbook and other governing documents.

In the end, senior administrators make the hard decisions about deploying and redeploying the school's limited resources (e.g., faculty "lines," physical space, and operating capital) in response to market forces, student interests, and internal capacities. The president should, on an annual basis, review with the Board the tactical allocation of resources and their strategic importance.

Facilitating Board Meetings (a.k.a. Herding Talented Cats)

Working with the president and Board professional, the chair ensures that meetings are strategic, efficient, and engaging. While there are moments for casual conversation and social interaction during Board dinners, designated breaks, and numerous social occasions outside of Board meetings, the plenary session and committee meetings should have clear agendas of important items with allotted times for each topic, and the chair should hold members and guests to the schedule.

Successful chairs and well-run meetings rely on the input of the Board professional who tracks important issues, incomplete discussions, and when and how these matters should be raised. Which trustee has been asked to give the opening prayer? Which new trustees and new senior administrators should be introduced to the assembly? What milestones should be celebrated, and what sad happenings should be acknowledged? The Board professional should assure that the chair has all of this at their fingertips.

All Board conversations can wander. The chair keeps the conversation on topic, gently guiding trustees to get to the point, deferring tangential comments to a later date, and ending the discussion when time or topic has been exhausted. The chair may also need to provide occasional, individual guidance to a trustee about how to present their ideas and what might be disruptive or offensive to others.

As you guide the Board through meetings, don't hesitate to make connections between agenda items, the strategic plan, the university's mission priorities, the comprehensive campaign, and other, larger frameworks.

When necessary, the chair should end the general discussion of an agenda item and say that the Board needs to move on. As experience with leading a Board grows, chairs find the mechanisms that work best for them and for the Board to keep advancing the agenda. Critical issues need time and anything that helps the Board spend more time on matters of consequence, and less on process and formality, is to the institution's benefit.

Best practices of well-run Boards include:

- Relying on a "consent agenda" that allows routine matters to be swept aside quickly; committee reports are sent ahead of time in the Board book rather than being reviewed at the meeting itself
- Beginning meetings with an executive session if important matters require Board-only time for thorough discussion
- Ending in a similar executive session — whether one is "needed or not" — allowing all trustees to speak freely when time permits. Board members often appreciate going around the table at the conclusion of a plenary session for quick (10-20 seconds) input from each trustee
- Asking the chief mission officer or another person to guide the Board in a five-minute Examen — a time-honored Ignatian spiritual practice — at the end of the Board meeting

Managing Difficult Board Conversations

Trustees' opinions may differ considerably when it comes to the nature, function, and authority of conscience — which is to say, how the school addresses moral or ethical issues. When crises erupt due to the actions of students or other members of the university community, the Board must appreciate the contours of the challenge and how university leadership has arrived at a response. Matters that involve Church teaching or concerns of the local bishop or Jesuit provincial may call into question university policies or procedures. In these cases, administration and the Board need to discuss the matter with intelligence and respect — respect for Church teaching or the bishop's/provincial's position and role, and respect for divergent positions among trustees. This can be a time of considerable tension on the Board, within the university community, or between the university and Church or Province authority. The chair has no easy job here. Several considerations can help guide the chair's approach to a Board discussion of the controversy.

1. First, there must be general agreement between the chair and president on the university's position or next steps. Until the president and chair have some general agreement, discussions with trustees or others should not take place.
2. Give the trustees a good grasp of the situation and its details. Have they received a clear explanation of the

university's position? Do they know the positions of other authorities, such as religious and civil authorities? Are there experts in moral theology or ecclesiology (i.e., Church law and procedure) who can explain the issues involved in the dispute? The Jesuits or a theologian on the Board can be helpful in explaining the issues at stake.

3. Avoid asking trustees to vote on a proposition, solution, or policy change. Voting leads to the perception of "winners and losers." The collective advice of the trustees may be something that arises from reflection on the conversation by the Executive Committee.
4. ***Do not be afraid to employ the resources of the Ignatian tradition and discerning practices in your discussions.*** For example, ask trustees to note any biases they may have about the topic. Consider what the Board will feel good about having done in five, 10, or 20 years. Take breaks for prayer and reflection. Assure that more reticent voices are heard. In many respects, the chair's role in mission governance is doubly important in this moment.
5. Once a consensus has been achieved at the Board level, someone should be deputized to explain the various positions and the consensus. The better the facts are relayed in total, the easier it is to affirm the consensus.
6. Trustees may be invited to add their thoughts after a meeting through email or other electronic means. Of

course, if the conversation is unusually rich and exceptionally fruitful, it is the chair's prerogative to extend the discussion at the cost of upcoming agenda items.

Fortunately, these situations are rare, but chairs are well advised to think about their own strengths in consensus-building and to ask for assistance in developing those skills.

Committees of the Board

Much of the important work of the Board happens in the committees. Working with the president, the chair and vice chair should carefully consider the assignments of trustees to committees where their expertise and dedication can bring maximum value to the university. An annual evaluation, including a self-evaluation, of each trustee's contributions to the good work of their committee(s) can be of great value to the chair for committee assignments and reassignments. The chair should maintain a three-year "look forward" plan for committee composition, including the prioritization of the recruitment of new trustees and maintenance of the culture of the Board so that divisions of labor and apportionment of responsibilities are respected and balanced.

Depending on the university's bylaws, committee chairs often form an Executive Committee (EC), which is under the leadership of the chair. A strong EC can serve as a valuable resource to the entire Board. The EC meets regularly with the president to receive updates on important matters and to offer advice and provide input on the selection of the next chair and vice chair(s). The selection of Board leadership should also be informed by input from the president, since these working relationships are so fundamental to institutional success. The scope of an EC is important, and the bylaws should clearly describe the extent and limits of their authority. Legal counsel can advise on appropriate language in the bylaws.

Ad hoc committees or task forces may, from time to time, be established to contribute perspective to the Board's oversight and deliberations. Created for a specific assignment that does not fit well within the purview of any one committee (e.g., searching for the next president, coordinating a comprehensive campaign, or reviewing and approving a revised mission, vision, and values statement), these temporary working groups have a clear assignment, a set membership, and an end goal, after which they are disbanded. Regarding the size and composition of such temporary groups, there is a creative tension between inclusion and efficiency — a broad membership will facilitate thorough input, and a small group will ensure efficiency and effectiveness.

Bylaws

The bylaws of the Board represent the most important statement of the organizational structure of the Board and its rules for operation, in addition to the United States Internal Revenue Code 501(c)(3) that establishes the institution's tax-exempt status, the applicable state's incorporation statute that may specify certain requirements for the bylaws, and the state's articles or charter of incorporation. Typically, the bylaws establish:

- Size of the Board
- Terms of office
- Membership rules and expectations
- Special classes of members, such as emeriti members
- Procedures for removal of members
- Designation of corporate officers, their selection, and responsibilities and authority
- Special rules for conducting meetings: designation of standing committees or how other standing or special committees shall be established if not otherwise specified in the bylaws
- Voting requirements, including special voting requirements for matters of particular importance
- Procedures for amending the bylaws

As noted, the bylaws may establish and provide the charge to each committee of the Board. These charges can and should be reviewed regularly by the committee membership, but suggested changes to the committee charge should only be made with the guidance and approval of the chair and approved in the manner provided by the bylaws. Beware of "mission creep," when one committee seeks to take on oversight that is properly the responsibility of another. Collaboration, based upon expertise and the good of the mission, is fine. Improper intrusion into another committee's charge is not helpful.

Working with the president and the Board professional (see page 31 for more information about this role), the chair should ensure that the Board is familiar with the bylaws and acting in compliance with them. Corporate counsel should be consulted regarding the meaning and purpose of articles in the bylaws, and, with the Board professional, should be counted upon for sound advice in questionable instances. If there are issues with a bylaw, the chair may wish to invite a Board member or the Governance Committee to lead a review of the specific bylaw in question, with input from appropriate committees, in order to bring recommendations to the Executive Committee and the eventual vote of the Board to amend the bylaws.

Annual self-evaluations by Board members support the chair's responsibility to see that all trustees are contributing their part in governing the university. Evaluations of the committee meetings and the meetings of the Board are also best practices. In addition, trustees are legally required to complete and sign conflict of interest forms for the IRS annually (see Appendix A for a sample conflict of interest policy). This helps to guarantee the credibility of a Board.

Recommended Resources

Book:

Trammell, J. (2016). *Effective board chairs: A guide for university and college chairs.* AGB Press.

Website:

Association of Catholic College and Universities website. https://www.accunet.org/trustees.html

Videos:

Association of Catholic Colleges and Universities. *Trustees in Catholic Higher Education: "Trust and Mission" (Part I, "Trust").* 2024. https://tinyurl.com/ACCUTrustVideo

Association of Catholic Colleges and Universities. *Trustees in Catholic Higher Education: "Trust and Mission" (Part II, "Mission").* 2023. https://tinyurl.com/ACCUMissionVideo

Chapter 2

Board Composition and Functioning

A healthy and well-functioning Board supports the university's mission at every level. It is the responsibility of the chair to leave the Board stronger, more impactful, and more consequential than they found it by importing the best practices of Board governance. These practices, suitably nuanced for the Board's culture, history, and circumstances, can modernize the Board and energize trustees. The Association of Governing Boards of Universities and Colleges (AGB) website – agb.org – contains a wide range of best practices for chairs, committees, and boards, and offers institutional consultations on request. Similarly, AJCU stands ready to support chairs in their work, and to help them learn about the best practices of other Jesuit institutions through network meetings and chair-to-chair conversations.

Board Membership

The Board chair leads the vetting and recruiting of new members, in partnership with the president. This is an essential element of a productive, efficient, and generative Board. It is a common governance practice for Boards to empower a standing committee to oversee these responsibilities. (e.g., a Committee on Trustees, a Nominating Committee, or a Governance and Nominating Committee). Such committees and their composition may also be mandated in the bylaws. The charge of these committees may vary depending on the Board's structure but, in all cases, certain core responsibilities are common: vetting, recruiting, nominating, and recommending new Board members.

The chair should take care to nominate or appoint an experienced trustee to lead this committee — or the chair may choose to lead the committee themselves. If the committee does not already have a charge in place, a review of the Board's past practices and bylaws will guide decision-making. The Nominating Committee should consist of well-respected trustees with several years of leadership experience on the Board, and of colleagues who have a nuanced understanding of governance, Board culture, and the competencies needed for healthy Board and committee functioning. Best practices promoted by the Association of Governing Boards of Universities and Colleges suggest that the Nominating Committee should be populated with the Board's best and brightest. When appointing the committee's membership, it is also important that members be attuned to the perceptions and feelings of the larger Board membership.

Ideal members have experience hiring and recruiting at the executive level, and those with a high emotional quotient (EQ) can assess whether a trustee candidate is temperamentally equipped to navigate challenges with composure and creativity. A potential trustee may, for example, not appreciate the time commitment required or may seek membership as a means to an expanded client base, rather than placing the institution's needs at the forefront.

Conflicts will arise from time to time but can be avoided at the outset with careful vetting.

Boards in the Jesuit network are generally self-sustaining. It is common to ask all Board members on a regular basis to submit nominees from their professional, civic, and social circles, and to provide them with a rubric and nomination form, listing all the relevant questions. Friends of the school who are already active on advisory boards or otherwise engaged may also emerge as potential trustees.

It is advisable for the president, chair, and perhaps the nominating trustee to meet informally with candidates and to meet again before extending an invitation to serve on the Board. Given the responsibility for the welfare of students, faculty, and staff, and the apostolic mission of the university, selecting new trustees is a weighty responsibility. The Board chair is charged in a unique way with seeing to the complementarity of talents, skills, and interests among trustees, and to the replacement of these qualities as trustees rotate off the Board. Further***, it behooves the Board chair to look to the diversity of the backgrounds of Board members so they reflect and inspire the whole community.***

When asking a candidate to serve on the Board, it is important to explain clearly the expectations that the university has for the trustee and the nature and scope of their commitment. Fiduciary duties and other commitments, such as mission formation, financial contributions, committee service, and attendance at meetings and Board functions, should be carefully explained. A letter of appointment after a Board vote should reaffirm these expectations.

Two words of caution are offered here. First, it is important to be very clear about conflicts of interest when recruiting a Trustee who is a current parent. The candidate must explicitly agree that they will allow their student to have a complete, wholesome, and normal college experience, free from any hint of undue parental interference. Similar clarity is necessary for trustees who are alumni. They must understand that history has continued apace as they grew older; the institution has evolved in important ways and will continue to change. As a trustee, it will be their co-responsibility to assure that the mission and identity of a contemporary Jesuit institution of higher education meets the moment.

Many Boards invite a potential Board member to serve as a non-trustee on a Board committee or on an institutional advisory board before inviting them to join the Board of Trustees. This allows both the candidate and university leadership to assess the interest in, and potential for, a good match.

When considering new Board members, the process for vetting ought to include an assessment of whether the candidate can contribute to the mission of a Jesuit and Catholic university.

Does the mission inspire and motivate this person? Does the potential trustee have a deep interest in how the university can benefit the community and its students, faculty, and staff precisely because it is a faith-based institution? This unpaid, voluntary seat on the institution's highest governing body ought not to become a trophy, a side interest, or even simply a civic duty. There is a great deal at stake in taking on responsibility for advancing the mission of education and service by a faith-based institution.

Recruiting Jesuit Trustees and Other Educators

Board bylaws typically include a designated number of Jesuit trustees. Provincials have asked that they be informed about the Board's desire for a Jesuit to serve before he is asked about his availability. They ***welcome the chance to suggest Jesuits who are available and whose skills and backgrounds mesh well with the Board's needs.*** Chairs may also wish to consult with current Jesuit trustees, asking them to nominate suitable Jesuit candidates who bring knowledge, experience, and commitment to this important fiduciary responsibility. A best practice, then, is for the president or chair to contact the local provincial regarding the request. If the Jesuit is interested and determined to be an apt trustee, the provincial superior will mission him to serve on the Board at the end of the recruitment process. All of a Jesuit's major apostolic commitments are subject to approval and missioning by the provincial.

In composing a healthy and effective Board, the Nominating Committee should consider the number of trustees with credentials in higher education: provosts, deans, and vowed religious from other congregations with higher education experience all fit this bill. A significant representation of education experts on the Board will inform discussions and lend depth to the Board, especially with respect to understanding the unique role that a Jesuit and Catholic university plays in the wider community. As a general rule of thumb, ***at least one quarter of the trustees should know the business of higher education through their own education and experience.***

The more time and deliberation that goes into selecting and vetting new trustees — and the more intentional the effort to recruit trustees who are well-acquainted and deeply interested in the mission — the better the outcomes for all.

Terms and Rotations

Ideally, trustee terms and term limits are set by the bylaws. The Board bids farewell to some members and welcomes new members annually. Periodic changes in leadership of committees and of the Board as a whole are healthy and necessary.

As valuable and loved as an individual trustee may be, eight or nine years of continuous service is a sufficient gift of wisdom, dedication, and prudential guidance — and this is for trustees who have proven themselves. Toward the conclusion of a trustee's term, a judgment must be made about whether or not they should be invited to serve for another term. If the trustee is not attending or participating in meetings, or if they are showing up unprepared, or if their interjections continue to reveal that they don't understand or support the mission, then they should be thanked and excused at the end of their term.

Trustee term renewal must not be automatic. It may be a very painful conversation, but the Board exists to guarantee the mission of the institution. In these difficult times, Boards must maximize their effectiveness, and they can only do this by maximizing their appropriation of the mission and identity of the institution.

Trustees Emeriti/ae

Over time, the regular rotation of Board membership builds a reserve of trustees emeriti, which is an honorific conferred for life upon some former trustees. Trustees emeriti may serve as mentors to new trustees, faculty, staff, and/or students. They are ambassadors to the alumni community, as well as to the public at large, and they may be engaged to consult on issues of expertise or to work on particular projects. After a break in Board service and subject to the bylaws, an institution may occasionally ask a former trustee to return for another term or two. This is appropriate if the former trustee possesses unique qualifications, but too much of this practice — or the lack of term limits — can lead to a Board that is stagnant and not optimally prepared to deal with the complexities and novelties of the current, shifting landscape of higher education.

Recommended Reading

Association of Governing Boards of Universities and Colleges. (2021). *Policies, practices, and composition of governing boards of colleges, universities, and institutionally related foundations.*

Board Member Terms - FAQ Guide (2020). Association of Governing Boards of Universities and Colleges. https://agb.org/ (Membership/login required)

Chapter 3
Meeting Protocols and Procedures

The success of any meeting begins with thorough preparation. Trustees should come prepared by carefully reviewing the agenda and supporting materials in advance — not only for their individual committee meetings but also for Board meetings. A carefully crafted agenda that is focused on meaningful and strategic issues is essential to an effective and well-received meeting. The more input gathered during the drafting of the agenda, the greater the level of Board engagement.

Board meetings should foster a safe and respectful environment where trustees feel empowered to contribute their insights, raise thoughtful questions, and provide constructive feedback in service of the school's mission.

While the Board ultimately acts as a unified body and speaks with one voice outside the boardroom, meetings themselves should allow space for open dialogue and even healthy debate.

Encouraging trustees to share differing viewpoints and to challenge proposals when necessary provides for robust discussion and strengthens the decision-making process. Each trustee was invited to serve on the Board because of their unique perspective, and it is through the collective wisdom of the group that the Board best fulfills its responsibilities.

Agenda Setting

The following components should be included on the standard draft agenda:

- Call to order
- Opening prayer and/or Ignatian Moment
- Approval of the consent agenda (including previous meeting minutes and other housekeeping matters)
- Chair's report
- President's report
- Informational and action items
- Executive session (as needed)
- Adjournment (may be preceded by an Ignatian Examen)

The agenda may also include:

- Current issues facing the university
- Regular reports (including enrollment progress, financial forecasts, and accreditation updates)
- Approvals that are on a recurring cycle (including approval of the operating budget and tuition and fee increases)
- Committee reports that merit the Board's attention (including a development or campaign update)

Timed meeting agendas should align with the highest-order objectives and goals of the university. Affording sufficient time and attention for relevant and important issues often means that other matters cannot be discussed, particularly at quarterly Board meetings. The president and the Board professional are essential resources for the preparation of a draft agenda. Collaborating with the Board professional will help map the work of a quarterly meeting, the principal topics of which were previously set in a year-long plan.

The Executive Committee should review a proposed agenda before it is distributed to the members of the Board. Long reports, too many topics, and too little discussion can lead to dissatisfaction among trustees whose insightful questions, considered opinions, and prudential judgments have no time to be aired. Many Boards today are attempting to reduce the amount of pre-reading materials. Shortening reports to include only essential points and placing reports in appendices can help to make Board reading material manageable.

Preparation and Distribution of Materials

The Board professional is a university staff member who works with university leadership to gather supporting documents for the agenda, provides additional information or context, and invites key individuals to present on the topic(s) at hand. The Board professional sends the materials to the Board members and other approved recipients at least seven days ahead of a meeting and/or notifies the membership when they may access materials through the Board's online portal. Speakers should plan to rehearse their presentations prior to the meeting to hone their messages and build upon the brief summaries included in the pre-meeting materials.

Conducting Meetings

A well-run meeting needs a set of agreed-upon practices so that individuals know how and when they can make their opinion known and how decisions will be voted upon and recorded. *Robert's Rule of Order* is a frequently used and trusted way to ensure that all participants feel their contributions are valued and that the process is equitable, efficient, and proper. How strictly a Board wishes to follow *Robert's Rules of Order* is a matter of the chair's preferences and the group's size.

> BoardEffect provides an overview of *Robert's Rules of Order*, practical tips, and a handy cheat sheet at https://tinyurl.com/RobertsRulesSheet.

University cultures vary with respect to how staff and Board members interact at Board meetings, but it is important to remember that Board meetings are for the Board. Staff expertise is invaluable to the Board. That being said, staff who are present serve as resources and not meeting participants. Staff may be called upon to present, facilitate a discussion on a dedicated topic, or respond to a question, but they ought not insert themselves, uninvited, into the Board's meeting. Some trustees can defer to the staff excessively, thereby abdicating their governance role.

Effective Board Practices

To keep trustees engaged, begin each meeting by giving a brief overview of the agenda and goals of the meeting. This helps participants stay focused on the meeting objectives. Time expectations are more easily managed by building the meeting timeline into the agenda and noting scheduled meeting breaks, especially for longer meetings. If using the traditional *Robert's Rules*, the chair should formally call for a vote to approve the agenda; this can be done before the approval of prior meeting minutes.

In the course of the meeting, encourage discussion and invite trustees to ask questions at the end of reports and presentations. It is the role of the chair — and not of those presenting — to field and queue questions and comments. The Board professional should inform presenters of this in advance to avoid any confusion. The chair should also directly involve quieter trustees by soliciting their opinions and feedback.

Other ideas to encourage participation:

- Invite trustees to download and view meeting materials on their personal devices
- Project the agenda on a large screen(s) in the meeting room
- Announce when moving on to the next agenda item

- Invite trustees to bring a device to take notes if meetings are paperless or provide a writing pad and pen at each seat to encourage note taking
- Ask presenters to create questions for each report or presentation to help initiate discussion when needed

If the bylaws provide for virtual participation by trustees, those who are online must be included as fully as possible. The Board professional can help by watching for questions and comments from the video platform and by serving as a liaison to them in the plenary or in breakout sessions.

Executive Session

Each Board meeting should include at least one executive session. These sessions are reserved exclusively for trustees, though the chair may invite select non-trustees to remain when appropriate. Executive sessions provide a confidential environment where trustees can engage in open, honest, and sometimes difficult conversations about sensitive or high-stakes matters. These sessions are essential for building trust, encouraging candid dialogue, and, when necessary, allowing space for disagreement. Importantly, while executive sessions promote transparency among trustees, they also foster unity. Once discussions conclude, the Board emerges with a shared perspective and speaks with one voice.

Including an executive session as a standing item on the agenda helps normalize its use and alleviates any discomfort or perceived pressure on individuals to request one.

During the course of the meeting, trustees may encounter agenda items that raise sensitive or confidential issues. In such cases, they should be advised to reserve these matters for discussion during the executive session. If, by that point, there are no confidential issues requiring further attention, the session can simply be omitted.

To ensure transparency and understanding, the Board professional will communicate proactively with faculty, staff, alumni, and student representatives about the purpose of executive sessions and the rationale for their exclusion from these portions of the meeting. Presidents are included in executive sessions only when invited by the chair.

Discussions held during executive sessions are not included in the official meeting minutes, as they are considered confidential and private to the membership. General counsel may be present, as needed, to ensure attorney-client privilege when legal matters are discussed. Any formal Board actions resulting from executive session deliberations must be voted on and approved during a regular session of the Board, where proceedings are recorded in the minutes. The chair is responsible for formally announcing both the commencement and conclusion of the executive session.

Following Up After Board Meetings: Minutes and Action Items

Minutes are critical to the integrity of the Board meeting discussion and final decisions. They are taken to ensure that motions and resolutions are accurately recorded but should not be a transcript of the debates that led to the final decisions. Minutes are considered to be very important historical documents for two reasons:

- *Decision-making:* It is imperative that the minutes accurately reflect the final decisions for each motion or resolution brought before the Board. These decisions become part of the record of the institution; they may be consulted years later, due to turnover among university and Board leadership or in legal matters. Minutes do not include decisions or discussions from outside the meeting. The decisions made by the Board are implemented by the president and university leadership.

- *Accreditation:*_All colleges and universities are subject to independent accreditation bodies, unique to their geographic region — WSCUC, HLC, SACSCOC, NEASC, etc. — or tied to a particular academic discipline such as ABA for Business schools and ABET for engineering programs. A key component of these accreditors' cyclical reviews includes assessing the Board minutes to ensure that the university is operating according to its bylaws. Additionally, each accreditation agency has its own accrediting standards, and they typically use Board minutes to determine whether the university is meeting these requirements.

Accountability mechanisms must be consistently upheld by both the Board and university leadership. These mechanisms can take various practical forms, including the following:

- Conducting regular Executive Committee meetings between the quarterly Board sessions to ensure timely updates, continuity, and responsiveness to emerging issues.
- Including an executive summary with each set of meeting minutes, highlighting key motions or resolutions passed. The summary should also feature an after action report that identifies responsible parties and outlines a proposed timeline for implementation. These items should be revisited at the beginning of the following meeting to ensure follow-through and transparency.
- Requesting post-meeting evaluations from Board members after each meeting. These evaluations are essential for assessing the effectiveness, clarity, and overall value of the meeting. Feedback collected can help identify areas for improvement, ensure that Board members feel heard and

engaged, and promote a culture of continuous improvement and shared accountability.

Recommended Reading

Legon, R. D. (2014, March/April). The 10 habits of highly effective board meetings. *Association of Governing Boards of Universities and Colleges*, *22*(2).

Robert III, H. M. (2020). *Robert's Rules of Order*. PublicAffairs.

Chapter 4

Financial Oversight and Stewardship

Board chairs need to develop a strong understanding of the institution's finances. While Catholic, Jesuit colleges and universities seek to serve all qualified students, few have the resources to meet all the financial needs of every student they admit. The Board as a whole, and especially the Board chair, has a fiduciary responsibility to ensure the institution's financial stability and, thus, to support its mission. This chapter offers a framework for Board chairs of AJCU institutions to oversee the university's financial matters effectively. By focusing on key areas, Board chairs can help ensure that their university remains financially healthy, mission-focused, and capable of achieving its strategic objectives.

Foundational Knowledge

The chair should be well-acquainted with the budget, budget process, institutional financial situation, and any financial issues the institution will be facing. Even when the chair possesses this expected level of familiarity, they will frequently find themselves in situations where credibility and effectiveness are more likely to require greater mastery of the institution's finances. For a new chair, it is important to ask the right questions of the right people. Respect for an incoming Board chair is always higher if the chair has learned the details of the institution's finances and operations, and has sought opinions and advice from trusted sources.

Important aspects of higher education's unique financing model include understanding the difference between operating and capital budgets, unrestricted versus restricted gifts, and endowment funds — and how each serves a different purpose within the institution. The various revenue sources, including tuition, philanthropy, endowment distribution, and research grants, together make up the institution's chief sources of income. Trustees will need to know if the trend line of revenue supports a financial model that is sustainable for the coming years. Board leadership, then, needs to focus on what needs to happen to achieve or strengthen financial security.

Critical Questions Asked by Effective Boards

- What are the total costs of student attendance by school/college and even by academic major?
- What is the net tuition revenue — factoring in the percentage of discount for student aid — by academic program type?
- What is the value of the endowment assets? How is the endowment value calculated?
- What is the institution's endowment spending policy, and is it being enforced?
- What is the annual operating and capital budget?
- How much is spent on teaching, student services, and administration? How does this breakdown compare with peer institutions?
- What is the institution's debt, as well as its capacity to add more or refinance debt?
- What are its financial and debt ratings?
- What is the school's practice for funding capital renewal and replacement? Does the current practice result in so-called "deferred maintenance," and what plans are in place to address it?

Understanding the University Budget

The Board is responsible for approving the annual budget. This involves reviewing the proposed budget, asking critical questions, and making informed decisions. Built on a forecast of future events, the university budget is the financial roadmap that reflects the institution's obligations, priorities, and strategic goals. ***Understanding the budget allows Board chairs to ensure that resources are allocated effectively to support the school's mission.*** It is important to familiarize yourself with the key components of the university budget, including (a) revenue sources, such as tuition, fees, grants, and donations, and (b) expenditure categories, including salaries, infrastructure, research, and student services.

The budgeting process — and the alignment of resources and strategic priorities — should reflect the school's overall Catholic and Jesuit mission, as well as the practice of shared institutional governance by faculty, staff, and administrators. *How* Jesuit schools conduct their budgeting processes reflects as much about them as the budgets they develop. The Board chair should encourage leadership to participate in this essential exercise conducted by the chief financial officers and others, designing or adjusting the budgeting process to be as inclusive and transparent as the work allows, and building reflection and honest conversation into each stage. With this in mind, best practices include:

- Establishing a timeline for budget approval that allows for thorough review and discussion
- Ensuring that the budget reflects a balanced approach, considering both immediate needs and long-term sustainability
- Engaging with the university's finance team to understand the assumptions and projections underpinning the budget

Risk Management, Audits, and Compliance

Risk management is rarely anyone's favorite topic and the risks to higher education are increasing on a range of fronts. Reputational risks, cyber risks, physical plant risks, and campus security risks are but a few of the categories that fall to the committee addressing issues of institutional risk. Germane to the financial realm, however, all trustees should be proactive in asking administrative leadership to identify potential financial risks — such as softening demand for admission, declining enrollment, or increased costs — and review with university leadership the institution's mitigation strategies. These topics, too, should be regular agenda items for the Risk Management Committee, whose members provide essential expertise for the Board.

To ensure compliance, universities undergo regular financial audits by independent external auditors. The Board chair should be familiar with the audit process and the resulting reports. If there is an office of internal audit, the Audit or Finance

Committee of the Board should receive regular updates from it and communicate these to the Board at large. It's a necessity to oversee the university's compliance with financial regulations, including federal and state laws and accreditation requirements. The chair, in consultation with the president, should work with the finance and legal teams to ensure adherence to these standards. Finally, ***the Board and Executive Committee need to support the development and maintenance of strong internal controls to prevent fraud and ensure the integrity of financial reporting.***

Monitoring the financial health of your school is best accomplished by including these three steps:

1. Regularly review key financial indicators, such as cash flow, endowment performance, debt levels, and operating margins at the degree or school level. Stay abreast of both annual and multi-year trends in admissions and enrollment management. These metrics provide insight into the financial health of the university.
2. Establish regular reporting intervals for financial updates. Ensure that the Board receives clear and concise reports from the finance team.
3. Set the tone for the Board and campus leadership to ensure that they see themselves as one team when reviewing financials.

Fundraising: Developing Resources

Board chairs play a crucial role in leading and supporting fundraising initiatives, particularly campaigns aimed at securing major gifts for specific projects or endowments. Working closely with the university's advancement office to set challenging yet realistic fundraising goals and strategies ensures Board buy-in. These efforts should be carefully aligned with the university's long-term strategic plan and mission priorities.

It is important, once again for credibility's sake, for a Board chair to demonstrate a personal commitment to fundraising by making significant contributions and encouraging fellow Board members to do the same. The chair can also foster strong relationships with major donors and promising alumni, particularly through personal networks. The role of chair includes being an ambassador for the university, communicating its vision and goals effectively. By thoughtful engagement, the alumni community has the opportunity to give back, both financially and through volunteer efforts. And, to this end, it is important to be seen and known as someone who participates in donor cultivation events and stewardship activities.

Endowment Oversight

The Investment Committee needs outstanding, experienced trustee leadership. Assure that they have set sound investment allocations guidelines, established appropriate benchmarks, and articulated an ethical investment policy that reflects the institution's Jesuit, Catholic identity. Among the investment categories that AJCU member schools avoid are weapons manufacturing, for-profit prisons, fossil fuel extraction and refinement, and manufacturing entities where human trafficking and child labor are rampant. Be sure to regularly review the university's social and ethical investment policy alongside other metrics and guidelines.

While specific policies vary, an annual distribution from the endowment of 4.5% of a three-year rolling market value average is now common. This allows for current funding of programs according to the wishes of the original philanthropists, while assuring the long-term growth of the corpus to yield intergenerational equity. Unrestricted gifts or funds whose original designation is no longer valid (e.g., scholarships for a degree program in telegraphy) should be repurposed by the Board for a similar good (e.g., scholarships for computer science students).

On occasion, Board chairs may have to intervene in cases where a trustee invites the institution to invest in their new venture. Even the appearance of a conflict of interest should be assiduously avoided. The president can deal with alumni who come forward with similar offers. Clear, published investment guidelines are helpful in sidestepping such potentially sticky matters.

Recommended Reading

Carnes, M., Hauver, D., Holiday, N., & Miciak, A. (2023, September 9). In conversation: Mission vs. money: Is it really an either or? *Conversations on Jesuit Higher Education*. https://tinyurl.com/MissionvsMoney

Laramee, W. A. (2024, July/August). Mountain fog: Reflections on the work of the finance committee. *Association of Governing Boards of Universities and Colleges, 32*(4).

Vitters, C. & Braunsdorf, J. (2023, September 20). *Risk governance in higher education: What boards of trustees need to know.* Deloitte Center for Government Insights. https://tinyurl.com/RiskGovernanceforBoards

Chapter 5

Strategically Planning for the Future

The chair of a Jesuit university Board is the chief conversation partner in the vital arena of strategic thinking and planning. This requires that the chair see themselves, the Board, and the university as dynamic and responsive entities. As the expression goes, "Only dead fish swim with the current." Each school must be able to navigate the different local and global currents surrounding it. As institutions sponsored by the Society of Jesus, Jesuit universities chart their course in the context of that partnership and with the aid of a recurring process called the Mission Priority Examen (MPE). This chapter offers some guidance on where to focus the Board's attention, which questions should be asked when it comes to strategic initiatives and innovation, and how to think about the school's future as a vibrant, sponsored apostolate of the Society of Jesus.

Strategic Planning

It is the president's role to establish a strategic plan. In creating the plan, some presidents consult widely across campus while others talk with key leaders within and beyond the institution. Whatever the process, the president ultimately sets before the Board the university's strategic plan — its Big Sky

Thinking. ***It is then up to the Board to approve, inspire, and monitor the speed and direction of innovation.***

The late, famed Jesuit preacher Walter Burghardt, S.J., was fond of predicating spiritual growth or wholeness on "a long, loving look at the real." Rooted in the Spiritual Exercises, this openness to the reality of our lives — not what we say about ourselves, but who we really are — is also the right starting point for discerning a Jesuit institution's future. The school will need data and metrics to begin an honest and accurate assessment of its present position — its academic standing, financial security, and involvement with the wider community, are but a few examples.

The school's senior leaders should provide background to the Board on the following questions, so that trustees are better prepared to exercise their role in strategic planning:

- Is there a recent academic portfolio review that shows not only all of the degree and certificate programs currently on offer, but also their net return on investment and recent trends?
- Are there opportunities for growth, and do these require investment?
- Have particular programs run their course, and should they be sunsetted so that resources can be redeployed elsewhere?

- What new market trends are on or beyond the horizon? In which of these could our institution make a strategic investment? In which would our institution have a distinctive niche?
- How do the school's mission priorities, established through the Mission Priority Examen process, factor into the institution's current commitments? How will they be incorporated into the strategic planning process?
- What do we know about student satisfaction, institutional climate, or the social mobility of first-generation graduates?

External conditions and internal capacities, whether latent or acquirable, need to be balanced, as does selecting a time horizon. Will the school chart a course for three, four, or five years? While the plan may be conceived of as a framework for the immediate future, in many ways strategic planning is a perennial exercise. The Board chair, working closely with the president, will review capabilities and progress on a regular basis. Selecting key metrics helps administrators know what the Board will expect and how their performance will be assessed.

Soft goals, like growing peer review rankings and strengthening student success, are laudable and vital, but they may be difficult to quantify and measure. They are achieved indirectly by making concrete progress towards much more mundane measures of headcount, net tuition revenue, degree completion, post-study employment in the chosen field, etc. If a particular degree program is flagging, it is the responsibility of academic leadership to fix or close the effort. If a program is doing well, can it do better?

Essentially, every higher education strategic initiative is based on four pillars:

- Mission — Does the initiative express the institution's Jesuit, Catholic mission?
- Revenue generation — Are enrollments robust, and is the initiative generating positive net revenue (taking into account physical and personnel investments)?
- Quality — Is the program moving toward national accreditation and/or positive external peer review for quality assurance?
- Relevance — Are graduates of the program making a positive impact on society?

Dreaming, inventing, planning, and executing new and revised academic programs is not so easy. Low-cost, online competition is rampant. ***Today, the value of a Jesuit, Catholic education needs to be demonstrated to convince students and parents to pay the hefty price of in-person (and hybrid) educational experiences.***

The process of strategic planning is tedious and lengthy, calling for both discipline and patience. Trustees contribute many talents to the effort. Their personal experiences at work and with workforce development can be extremely beneficial to the process.

Compensation and Succession Planning

In keeping with IRS standards and higher education best practices, Boards should include a Compensation Committee among trustee responsibilities. This committee will oversee the compensation and succession planning of the administrative leadership team. The committee will regularly review the total compensation packages of the "disqualified employees," an IRS term that signifies officers of a nonprofit, tax-exempt corporation who control significant amounts of money, personnel, and decision-making, or who are closely related to them, or whose compensation package is among the 15 highest at the institution. The Compensation Committee will also likely play a significant role, along with the Executive Committee and the Board, in the regular evaluation of the president, as specified by the Bylaws.

The Board chair will likely be an ex officio member of the Compensation Committee and thus will add to committee discussions important perspective on the president's effectiveness and satisfaction. Succession planning should be an annual topic of conversation between the chair and the president, both in regard to the senior leadership team (i.e., the vice presidents) and the president. For a president wishing to wind down their term, the chair can serve as a co-discerner regarding timing and a graceful transition.

A series of trustees may serve as Board chair during the career of a president, though presidential tenures have become shorter in recent years. The era in which a president remained in office for 25 years is likely over. Board chairs should therefore be attentive to signs that the president is nearing the end of their tenure and use their privileged relationship with the president to assure a graceful transition whenever possible.

Jesuit Sponsorship and the Mission Priority Examen (MPE)

The university does not plan in a vacuum. It does so while honoring its responsibilities to accrediting bodies, academic norms, students, families, and the needs of local, national, and global communities. A Jesuit university also has obligations related to the Society of Jesus and the Catholic Church. As a Jesuit-sponsored institution, the university's planning must be deeply informed by the Society's mission and by the Universal Apostolic Preferences that guide all Jesuit works:

Society of Jesus' Universal Apostolic Preferences

- **Showing the way to God** through the Spiritual Exercises and discernment
- **Walking with the excluded**, the poor, the outcasts of the world, and those whose dignity has been violated, in a mission of reconciliation and justice
- **Journeying with youth** and accompanying young people in the creation of a hope-filled future
- **Caring for our common home** and collaborating with gospel depth for the protection and renewal of God's creation

Through the Mission Priority Examen (MPE), the Society of Jesus and AJCU invite the whole university community to reflect on how effectively it integrates Jesuit values into:

- Leadership and public commitment to the mission
- The academic life
- The pursuit of faith, justice, and reconciliation
- Promoting an Ignatian campus culture
- Service to the Church
- Relationship to the Society of Jesus
- Institutional integrity

Based on the reflective practice of the Ignatian Examen, the MPE process guides the campus community to discern mission priorities that will inform institutional decision making, and that should be integrated into strategic planning, budgeting, and other direction-setting efforts. By discerning and committing to Jesuit mission priorities, the college or university strengthens its partnership with the Society of Jesus and demonstrates its commitment to Jesuit higher education in the years to come.

Questions Underlying the MPE

- What makes a college or university Jesuit?
- What does Jesuit sponsorship of a college or university require today?
- How will all AJCU member institutions and associate members live our Jesuit, Catholic mission now and in the future?

The Board chair's role in the MPE process is critical in ensuring that the university remains faithful to its Catholic identity and Jesuit mission, while also adapting to contemporary challenges. Much more than a procedural review, the MPE is a moment for engaging in deep, university-wide reflection, strengthening the school's relationship with the Society of Jesus, and setting clear priorities for living the mission with intentionality.

The MPE Process

The MPE provides every AJCU school with a spiritually grounded framework for self-examination and the chance to ask big questions around purpose and impact in the world. A 12- to 18-month process brings the best fruits of the Jesuit Examination of Consciousness (i.e., the Examen) to an entire institution:

- The president appoints a self-study chair(s) to lead the MPE process and that chair, in turn, names a campus self-study committee.
- Guided by the self-study committee, groups of faculty, staff, students, and trustees reflect on areas of institutional mission strength and areas for growth.
- Using the foundational document, *Characteristics of Jesuit Higher Education: A Guide for Mission Reflection,* as their compass, the self-study committee writes a report, recommending to the president two or three mission priorities for the school's next seven years. Each of these major priorities may have sub-priorities within it.
- A peer visitor team composed of experienced colleagues from other AJCU schools visits the college or university and writes a peer team report with their impressions and recommendations. The peer team report is written in a frank, collegial manner, focusing on the well-being and mission authenticity of the school engaged in the MPE.

- After making any needed adjustments to the self-study or peer team report, all documents are submitted to the local provincial superior and to the AJCU president. As a group, the provincials discuss each school engaging in an MPE that year.
- Letters on each institution's MPE are written by the local provincial, president of the Jesuit Conference of Canada and the U.S., and president of AJCU to the Jesuit superior general. The submissions to the superior general also include the self-study and the peer team report.
- The superior general reviews all materials and makes a decision about whether to reaffirm the Jesuit and Catholic identity of the college or university.
- The president receives word of the superior general's reaffirmation and recommendations from the local provincial and shares the outcome with the campus community.

The Board's Role in the MPE

The Board chair plays a key leadership role in guiding the Board's participation in the MPE and ensuring that the process is engaged as a strategic priority. The chair's responsibilities include:

- Understanding the MPE framework and talking with the Board about the MPE as a spiritual and practical experience

- Familiarizing the Board with *Characteristics of Jesuit Higher Education: A Guide for Mission Reflection* and explaining how its main points are reflected in the university's governance, financial decisions, academic programs, and student formation
- Promoting proper trustee engagement in the MPE process, encouraging active participation from Board members in the self-study focus groups and the site visit by the peer visitor team
- Providing strategic oversight and working with the president and the Mission Committee of the Board to align Board-level decision-making with the university's mission priorities
- Guiding the Board to review and approve the self-study before it is submitted to the local provincial and AJCU president
- Overseeing the president's implementation of priorities that arose through the MPE process — Like all assessment exercises, the MPE assumes continuous improvement. Provincial assistants for higher education visit the schools annually to discuss progress toward the mission priorities.

Follow-up

Once the president receives word of the superior general's reaffirmation of the school's Jesuit mission and Catholic identity, the Board should monitor progress on key mission initiatives, incorporate the priorities into strategic planning and presidential evaluations, and support mission-focused efforts, including faculty/staff formation, diversity and inclusion efforts, and community partnerships.

The Mission Priority Examen is an opportunity for trustees to reaffirm the Jesuit character — and therefore the Catholic identity — of the school and ensure that it remains a mission-driven institution well into the future. The chair's leadership will help sustain and strengthen this identity at the highest levels of governance. Chairs should not hesitate to reach out to fellow trustees at other Jesuit institutions who can provide insight on how they best integrated the MPE into the work of the Board — and how many are using it for ongoing Board formation.

Recommended Reading

Association of Jesuit Colleges and Universities. (2021). *Characteristics of Jesuit higher education: A guide for mission reflection.* https://tinyurl.com/CharacteristicsofJHE

Association of Jesuit Colleges. and Universities. (n.d.). *Mission Priority Examen (MPE).* https://tinyurl.com/AJCU-MPE

Attis, D. (2023, August 28). *Most strategic plans fail to set useful goals. Why these mistakes make it impossible to meet institutional objectives.* EAB. https://tinyurl.com/StrategicPlanGoals

Butler, L. (2006). *The board's role in strategic planning.* Association of Governing Boards of Universities and Colleges. https://tinyurl.com/BoardRolePlanning

Eckel, P., & Trower, C. (2019). Strategy, higher education and boards (and forget planning). In P. D. Eckel & C. A. Trower (Eds.), *Practical wisdom: Thinking differently about college and university governance* (Chapter 14). Routledge.

Russell, S. (2023 Fall). Getting more from your MPE: New tools for trustees. *In Fides. (1),* 26-30. https://tinyurl.com/InFidesFall2023

Society of Jesus. (2019). *Universal apostolic preferences of the Society of Jesus.* https://www.jesuits.global/uap/

Chapter 6
The Board and the World of Faculty

Faculty career paths and traditions can seem like strange terrain to trustees who inhabit the corporate world. It is not unusual for those new to the Board to bemoan that "everything takes so long" and that the consultation process needed for good governance includes too many faculty voices, especially on matters central to the academic project. But the Board and faculty can find the right balance to work together effectively and accomplish their school's mission.

The American Association of University Professors states that shared governance relies on "an inescapable interdependence among governing board, administration, faculty, students, and others. The relationship calls for adequate communication among these components, and full opportunity for appropriate joint planning and effort." This chapter seeks to demystify some parts of the world of faculty and how that world intersects with the work of the Board.

Shared Governance

Shared governance is inherited from an earlier time and is forever evolving in concept and practice. In some respects, it bears a resemblance to corporate models known as "flat hierarchies" or "worker-driven strategies." The main enterprises of Jesuit colleges and universities are the education of students and the creation of new knowledge. To this end, the ***faculty are essential partners and drivers in the accomplishing school's mission.***

As described earlier, universities that historically were run by the Jesuit community and Province took on, over time, the shape and characteristics of other American universities, reflecting faculty-led, institutional governance. Today, faculty responsibility is centered on academic matters, though some among their ranks assume that faculty will remain central to a broad swath of university decision-making. This expectation frames, in part, the academic versus administrative tensions present in higher education today. Think, for example, about faculty votes of no confidence and the faculty's power to remove a president. Nothing quite like this exists in the average corporation.

When striking a balance in shared governance, the central question is, "Who decides what?" The administration, whose authority is delegated by the Board, is ultimately responsible for everything: the allocation of scarce resources (budgeting); the launch, maintenance, and closure of degree programs; the construction and maintenance of physical facilities; campus safety and well-being; student recruitment and enrollment; discipline of students; conferring of degrees; alumni relations; fundraising; plus all of the legal and regulatory matters that pertain to modern higher education. Since the university is still a Jesuit work with responsibility for the mission entrusted to the Board of Trustees, the administration and Board have a particular charge to assure mission integration and maintain a healthy relationship with the Society of Jesus. Chapter 5 of this *Guide* explains the process by which that is regularly assessed.

With such an extensive list of university functions and responsibilities, shared governance is not solely a partnership between faculty and Board. Many of the university's divisions are accountable to other entities through professional guidelines, codes of conduct, and civil laws in ways that affect shared governance. The Americans with Disabilities Act, for example, goes to the heart of the classroom experience, addressing equal educational access and participation for students with disabilities. Thus, senior administrators have full and final authority over many academic and operational matters, including the allocation of resources.

That being said, faculty retain some distinct and significant areas of authority and responsibility. Chief among these is the faculty's responsibility for the curriculum and especially the university core curriculum that transcends undergraduate colleges and disciplines. Changing the core can be a protracted and difficult process, and departmental territoriality can play a part. Faculty who are passionate about the core curriculum most often recognize it as the anchor and hallmark of a Jesuit higher education that it is intended to be. Whether they are vigorously defending a traditional core or striving to make the core more responsive to current needs, faculty are engaging in "mission talk" at a very deep level. Curricular decisions of all kinds are faculty work that Boards must trust them to undertake.

Individual faculty members may speak out and claim a right to express controversial opinions, which can be disconcerting at times to those who are focused on the reputation of the university in particular circles. It is therefore important for campus leaders to engage in broad consultation in decision-making — both to disseminate facts and information and to cultivate informed constituents who will explain and support significant presidential or trustee decisions among their faculty colleagues.

This wide consultation — an expression of shared governance — can slow down decisions as additional voices are drawn into the dialogue through a maze of meetings. Nonetheless, a Board chair can take heart in knowing that a thorough process, consistent with the culture of the university, has taken place. To reinforce the commitment to governance, a chair may want to ask Board members, "Have we consulted widely in a way that recognizes the value of our constituent bodies and our partners in mission?"

Academic Freedom

The concept and practice of academic freedom is a vital source of strength for Jesuit higher education institutions, and exercising academic freedom plays a part in shared governance.

The protection of faculty members to discover and create new knowledge, as well as to teach established knowledge to their students without political interference or censorship, is an invaluable good that must be protected. Academic freedom has long been a bulwark against tyranny, with its roots stretching back to medieval European universities. Academic freedom guards against any political interference with or censorship of innovative ideas. The task of validating or debunking proposed discoveries falls to the peer review process by expert faculty members. Trustees are rarely involved in creating or enforcing rules to prevent, detect, and punish research malfeasance.

What remains contested is the breadth of a faculty member's right to say or write whatever they think outside their field of expertise. The U.S. Supreme Court's 2006 decision in the matter of *Garcetti v. Ceballos* left open for now the extent to which academic freedom pertains to faculty speech beyond their subject matter and research expertise. Until there is clarification in the courts, the local expectations of collegiality and professionalism are the important and ongoing task of faculty, administration, and trustees, all against the backdrop of the Catholic identity and Jesuit mission of the school.

In the United States, the Association of Governing Boards of Universities and Colleges' definition of academic freedom, and the American Association of University Professors' agreement with it, are the bedrock upon which the teaching and research programs of American schools are built. Academic freedom is also a major reason that the American higher education sector is the most productive in the world in terms of basic and applied research, scientific discoveries, and applications of these insights across industries and sectors. Faculty are free to pursue difficult and controversial lines of research and to express new theories within their field of research, especially in academic journals.

Advancing Faculty in Rank and Tenure

When considering a tenure decision or possible promotion or reviewing a double-blind, peer review of a manuscript, faculty are obliged to offer their opinions and judgments about the quality of their peers' teaching, scholarship, and service. They are similarly charged with a candid, professional assessment of student learning. They are expected to promote the ideals of their own learned societies (i.e., the national or international bodies of scholars of a particular discipline) and of the academy in general. These amount to both responsibilities and rights, such as a right to be judged by one's peers for misconduct, for salary increments, and for certain departmental or school positions, as well as for promotion and tenure. All of these duties and privileges are spelled out in the institution's faculty manual or handbook, a compendium of policies and practices of the academy.

Tenure and Promotion Process

New faculty members who recently earned a Ph.D. or similar degree usually have six to seven years to earn tenure, which means job security for the duration of their career unless the institution can show evidence of misconduct or financial exigency. All higher education institutions review a faculty member's progress toward meeting the department's standards and expectations for teaching and advising, student teaching evaluations, the scholarly record (e.g., the number of peer-reviewed publications), and the faculty member's record of service, both internal and external to the school. Each discipline and college/school further develops its own standards as they are germane to the field.

Around the halfway point of the tenure period, faculty go through a midterm review that includes the submission of a portfolio with examples of their work, external evaluations, student feedback, and personal statements about their teaching, research, and service. This review provides them with feedback on what will be needed if they are to continue on the path to achieving tenure. Those who move forward are again reviewed at the six- to seven-year point by a series of committees, the dean, and the provost, before the university president makes the final decision. Faculty who are unsuccessful in earning tenure at the end of their six- to seven-year "tenure clock" typically may stay one more year before leaving the university.

Alongside tenure-track faculty, there are also full- and part-time instructors who typically focus on teaching rather than research. These instructors often bring valuable real-world experience to the classroom and help guide students through internships. Their titles and roles can vary depending on the school, but they are frequently referred to as adjunct, clinical, or limited term.

Faculty Areas of Authority and Responsibility

Shared governance recognizes and takes into account the responsibility and capacity of the faculty to participate in important decisions regarding pedagogy, curriculum, research, and creative products, as well as evaluating individual faculty performance. Faculty committees devoted to various aspects of this important function (including departmental curriculum and school/college-level committees) absorb enormous time and energy. This is often an unrecognized contribution of faculty who prepare classes, teach, advise, publish, and serve on departmental, school, and university-wide committees — and who represent the university when presenting their work at national or international meetings in their field. Further, faculty cooperate with one another to support students in their efforts to successfully complete their degree program, take advantage of the co-curricular opportunities that help them develop leadership skills like cooperation and self-confidence, and assist them with the important questions that a life of faith and fidelity will raise.

Depending on the faculty's academic degree program, they must be vigilant in staying current on national standards and licensure requirements. Under the guidance of their academic dean and provost, they are responsible for the regular revision and continuous improvement of their academic courses and curriculum. Periodic external reviews by accreditors and academic rankings will judge their work.

For disciplines that do not have national standards, faculty and administrators are nevertheless responsible for meeting the quality standards of higher education and Jesuit institutions when it comes to the integrity of both curriculum and pedagogy — what is taught, how it is taught, and the resulting development of critical thinking, subject knowledge, and expressive skills. These standards are regularly assessed by regional accrediting bodies. Staff members and students will also have a voice in such accreditations; so, in certain important matters, they too share in governance.

Perhaps the most significant way in which the Board and the faculty intersect is by exercising their respective roles in advancing the quality of the university's educational programs and by promoting its Jesuit, Catholic mission. Here the faculty's role in hiring is paramount. The university is served best when the mission is addressed with faculty candidates at every level of the hiring process — from provost to dean to department chair to the departmental hiring committee — and when it is presented as a significant part of what the university, school, and department are all about. That is, what we teach, how we teach, and what questions we address in our courses are rooted in a faith that sees creation as a gift, as redeemed, and as a work-in-progress. The Jesuit university then fulfills its mission when it functions as a social enterprise, engaged with the world and especially with those on the margins — what Fr. Arturo Sosa, S.J., superior general of the worldwide Society of Jesus, calls a *proyecto social* for "reconciling the world to its Creator and to one another."[2] Can this new faculty member contribute to the university's Jesuit mission, envisioned in this way?

It is the faculty's part to exercise their essential governance responsibility both within their home institution and beyond its confines as regards the hiring, tenure, and promotion of their colleagues, the peer review of the academic work, and creative activity of their fellows across the academy. And it is equally their role to undertake the project of Jesuit higher education with an eye to its fundamental purpose of advancing "the service of faith and the promotion of justice." The Board must provide whatever support is necessary to support the faculty in this effort.

Recommended Reading

American Association of University Professors. (1966). *Shared Governance.* https://www.aaup.org/our-programs/shared-governance

American Association of University Professors. (1940). *Statement of Principles on Academic Freedom and Tenure with 1970 Interpretive Comments.* https://tinyurl.com/AAUP-AFandTenure

Association of Governing Boards of Universities and Colleges. (2017). *AGB Board of Directors Statement on Shared Governance.* https://tinyurl.com/AGB-SharedGov

Garanzini, M.J. (2023, Fall). The responsibilities of trustees at Jesuit institutions: A brief history. *In Fides. (1),* 7-15. https://tinyurl.com/InFidesFall2023

Sosa, A. (2018). *The University as a Source of Reconciled Life.* https://tinyurl.com/UniversityandReconciliation

Chapter 7
Legal and Ethical Responsibilities

The Board chair plays a critical role in ensuring institutional adherence to legal and ethical standards. This responsibility includes oversight of institutional compliance with federal, state, and local laws, as well as upholding institutional policies and values. The Board chair is responsible for confirming that trustees understand and observe their fiduciary duties and key corporate documents, comply with regulatory rules and accreditation standards, and meet the ethical expectations of the institution and the law. This includes active oversight of the following: risk management practices, compliance programs, and promotion of transparency and accountability at all levels of governance.

In all of these efforts, the chair should remember that the Board's lawyer — usually an in-house general counsel — is the lawyer for the corporation embodied by its Board. The chair should rely on the general counsel for institution-specific advice relating to all aspects of what is explained in this chapter.

Corporate Governance

Colleges and universities are fundamentally nonprofit, corporate entities. Typically they function as 501(c)(3) nonprofit corporations operating under the auspices of the state in which they are situated. This means that their articles of incorporation and bylaws control how the governing Board is composed.

Articles of incorporation establish the institution and its core organizational tenets, while bylaws control the institution's governance structure. The Board's resolutions and declarations — approved according to the procedural terms of the bylaws — describe formal actions taken by the Board. The policies, rules, and regulations adopted by the Board through resolutions serve as the broad parameters and operating guidelines that prescribe the institution's day-to-day operations. Sometimes, the Board has an additional layer of guidance in the form of internal operating procedures.

Board Fiduciary Duties

Every corporate Board and its individual members are legally obligated to exercise certain fiduciary duties. Although the characterization and composition of trustees' fiduciary duties vary slightly by state, there are three commonly described primary duties: care, loyalty, and obedience to the institution. Some experts include the duties of confidentiality, prudence, and disclosure as additional fiduciary duties, but those can also be considered subsets of these primary duties:

Fiduciary Duties

- Duty of care: The duty of the Board and trustees to act with the level of care, diligence, and competence necessary to make informed judgments for the institution, and to ensure decisions are made in good faith to support the institution's mission and mitigate risks
- Duty of loyalty: The duty of the Board and trustees to prioritize the institution's interests above personal gain, to avoid conflicts of interest, and to act with integrity to uphold the institution's mission
- Duty of obedience: The duty of the Board and trustees to ensure that the institution adheres to its mission, complies with applicable laws and regulations, and follows its governing documents and policies, thereby safeguarding the organization's purpose and public trust

To help Board members fulfill these duties, the Board chair must make sure Board members understand they are duty-bound to verify that funds are expended in support of, and to advance, the institution's mission in accordance with its values — what is known as financial stewardship or financial oversight. This involves:

- Implementing a mechanism to monitor and mitigate potential and actual conflicts of interest (typically a conflict of interest policy informed by IRS Form 990)

- Administering Board evaluations
- Overseeing implementation of the institution's whistleblower policy

Additionally, responsible Boards review institutional executives' compensation as part of their obligation to ensure that total compensation is not excessive and that the institution maintains its tax-exempt status. Hopefully, Board members received a thorough treatment of these obligations in a Board orientation. This orientation would be state-specific and would establish a common framework of these obligations among the trustees.

Regulatory Requirements and Compliance

Institutions of higher education that receive federal funds — which includes nearly all legitimate higher education institutions — are subject to a comprehensive framework of federal laws and regulations addressing federal financial aid, civil rights, campus safety, labor and employment, tax compliance, and research. Key laws include Title IX, the Clery Act, the Americans with Disabilities Act, Section 504 of Rehabilitation Act of 1973, and the Higher Education Act. These laws ensure non-discrimination, transparency in campus safety, and oversight of federal student aid programs.

Institutions must also comply with the Family Education Rights and Privacy Act (FERPA) to protect student privacy, and employment laws such as Title VII of the Civil Rights Act. Although day-to-day responsibility for legal compliance generally falls with the institution's general counsel, the Board and its chair are responsible for overseeing regulatory compliance as part of their obligation to protect the institution and act in its best interest.

Accreditation

Accreditation is a non-governmental, often regional or national, process for ensuring that an institution of higher education meets established standards of quality in such areas as academic rigor, student outcomes, faculty qualifications, and institutional resources. Accreditation provides a mechanism for quality assurance, accountability, transferability of credits, and eligibility for federal funding.

Although they are not involved in the details of the accreditation process, Boards work with their institution's president and chief academic officers (often a provost, academic vice president, or chancellor) to oversee the institution's alignment with accrediting bodies' standards and regulations, review and approve self-study reports, allocate resources to accreditation, and ultimately ensure that the institution will maintain its accreditations, which are vital to its continued viability. Boards may take a more critical look at these functions if an accreditation problem arises that threatens the academic health and reputation of the institution. The chair should lead the Board in the careful balance between heightened oversight and managing the problem, which should be left to university leadership.

Attorney-Client Privilege

Although the rules of privilege vary from state to state, the attorney-client privilege generally protects the confidentiality of communications between an attorney and their clients. ***In the case of an institutional entity, the institution's lawyers (such as its general counsel) owe their duties of responsibility and privilege to the institution itself, as opposed to any individual.*** When a trustee, especially the Board chair, seeks advice from the institution's counsel in their role as Board chair or trustee, their communications are generally privileged, subject to certain exceptions, such as when there is no expectation of privacy. However, most institutions ask their general counsels to offer their perspective on a broad range of business and policy matters outside of technical, legal advice. When counsel is acting outside of the role of the lawyer or in an administrative capacity, their communications with trustees or the Board chair are not privileged. Furthermore, merely adding counsel to a list of email recipients will not ensure that the communication is protected under the attorney-client privilege. If the chair is at all unclear on this matter, it will be important to ask the general counsel.

Document Retention and Electronic Discovery

If the Board has its own document retention policy, the chair should oversee compliance with this policy and abide by its timelines for retention and destruction. Certain documents — including those related to Board meetings and real estate transactions — are generally kept permanently. Additionally, the Board and Board chair must keep all documents relating to any matter in litigation. Destruction of such documents may be illegal. Prior to any such destruction, the chair or impacted Board member should contact the general counsel.

Litigation rules require institutions to produce all requested records, including electronic records. As a result, there may be times when legal counsel will, upon receipt of a complaint or demand, implement a "litigation hold" on all relevant records, which may include records possessed by Board members. For this reason, ***trustees are advised to use an institutional email address, so they can easily sequester relevant documents.*** The Board chair should oversee trustees' compliance with counsel's litigation holds.

Lawsuits and Ethical Conduct

When a higher education institution is sued, its counsel will perform a delicate calculation regarding how much it will cost to defend the suit. Experienced counsels are usually equipped to estimate the time, money, and reputational costs that may be required. Because the judicial system is biased toward settlement, given the expense of litigation, Board chairs should be prepared to hear the advice of counsel on the prospects of both defense and settlement when they confer with legal counsel about cases on their institution's litigation docket.

Boards and their chairs are also vested with authority and responsibility to ensure the institution's consistent commitment to certain non-legal, but no less critical, ethical obligations. One of the foremost ways the Board and chair do this is through the previously mentioned conflict of interest standards and disclosures required by the IRS, as well as by upholding the institution's Jesuit values.

Conflict of Interest Policies

Conflict of interest disclosure requirements should be codified in a Board conflict of interest policy, which should be based on the IRS Form 990. ***IRS Form 990 requires annual conflict of interest disclosures by all Board members, senior officers, and officials with significant responsibilities for management of institutional funds and assets, as well as their close family members who are employed by or in business relationships with the institution.***

A Board member who has a business relationship with the institution should disclose this in advance and refrain from participating in matters relating to the relationship by abstaining from voting and communicating regarding the matter. These and any other procedures should be spelled out in the Board's conflict policy. The chair should direct the Board's review of conflicts that are disclosed, as well as the IRS Form 990 before it is submitted to the IRS. However, the entire Board should have access to the IRS Form 990. Please see Appendix A for an example of key elements of a conflict of interest policy.

Upholding Jesuit Values

Jesuit institutions of higher education have an arguably higher standard for ethical conduct than do other institutions of higher education. Led by the chair, the Board should ensure that all of the institution's operations and its high-level strategic direction align with the institution's Jesuit mission and foster a campus culture that upholds the dignity of all individuals and a commitment to justice and the greater good. By actively engaging with the institution's mission, Jesuit college and university Boards and their chairs ensure that their governance reflects the spiritual and intellectual heritage of Jesuit education.

Recommended Reading

Auritt, R. (2024, September 17). *Why a conflict of interest policy is essential for nonprofit boards.* https://tinyurl.com/Conflict-Policy

Chapter 8

Crisis Management and Communication

An institution must be prepared for a broad spectrum of crises, including natural and human-made disasters, threats, and emergencies. Ensuring the campus is both secure and resilient is the responsibility of senior management with the oversight of, and perhaps assistance from, the members of its governing Board. The Board chair is uniquely positioned to support the president and senior administration as they work to prevent, protect against, mitigate, respond to, and recover from threats and crises — whether they are physical, digital, or reputational.

Crisis Preparedness

The administration should develop and regularly update plans for a wide variety of eventualities. Given the location of the school and shifting climate conditions, plans should be in place for natural disasters. Fires, floods, earthquakes, unusually heavy rain or snow storms, and similar occurrences can cause a campus to exercise extraordinary measures. Campuses never truly close, given that they may house students, have research labs with live animals, and certainly have physical resources to protect. The Board chair, working perhaps with an audit committee, should ensure that management has current disaster and crisis preparedness plans. The chair should relay advice or expertise on how to prepare for and respond to likely crises when they arise. This advice may come from internal expertise in the form of crisis teams or external consultants, or both. ***All institutions should be ready to take care of their own students, faculty, and staff; some may be called upon to care for their neighbors as well.*** AJCU schools met the moment in this regard when many welcomed students from Loyola University New Orleans to their campuses after Hurricane Katrina ravaged the city of New Orleans.

Whether through the Risk Committee, Audit Committee, Finance Committee, Executive Committee, or another committee of the Board, the chair should lead a subset of trustees in regularly ensuring that management is current with its crisis preparedness.

Enterprise Risk Management Plans

An effective tool for Boards to stay abreast of the risks posed to their campus is an enterprise risk management plan, or ERM, which can take several forms. Common among them, however, is a comprehensive definition of risk accompanied by an equally comprehensive listing of those risks across campus. The list includes the owners of each risk and some form of grading system. The system could be a heat map or a traffic light evaluation that considers the likelihood of the risk and the impact, should the risk materialize.

These plans are often housed within the purview of the Audit Committee. They provide a comprehensive guide to threats and opportunities — think of the broad definition of risk that includes opportunity — and a sense of the mitigation plans put in place by management. The plans are particularly effective in helping the Board oversee the operation of a university in light of the real threats posed by such issues as cybersecurity and active shooters.

An ERM plan will include topics such as the impact of political changes at home and abroad, wars and rumors of war, environmental degradation, and climate change. These and other matters can become contested issues on campuses, leading to protests, encampments, and demands on the administration to adopt certain policies or boycott specific entities. It is essential that before crises arise, the administration has foreseen these threats and has enacted campus policies and student conduct codes, and built good relationships with civil authorities. If these topics are not included in an institution's ERM plan, trustees should work with administration to address them.

The Board, under the leadership of the chair, should assure itself that risk management and crisis preparedness best practices are in place and aligned with both legal requirements and the institution's mission. ***Trustees should generally refrain from intervening in a crisis unless asked to do so by the president.*** Board members should certainly be kept informed but, in the main, the only Board action during a crisis would be the removal of the president for gross incompetence or malfeasance. Otherwise, the

Board supports the president and the leadership of the institution as they deal with the crisis. Issues of reputational harm, which fall within the scope of the Board, will be dealt with later in this chapter.

Reputational Risks

In addition to the previously mentioned emergencies, there are reputational risks that must be mitigated. Among the risks that consistently damage an institution's reputation are sexual assault, especially preventable assault; incompetent investigations and questionable resolutions; gross financial mismanagement and/or embezzlement; or an athletics scandal. Given the shifting landscape of collegiate athletics, some Boards at institutions with prominent athletics programs have established an Athletics Oversight Committee.

In all things, but especially in dealing with crises, an open, trusting, and respectful relationship between the Board chair and president is critical. A healthy relationship allows both to have difficult but productive conversations before, during, and after an incident. This is particularly important given the special relationship the chair has with the president. Keep in mind the lonely spot occupied by the president, particularly when the leadership team may be part of the problem. ***In times of crisis, the chair is a valuable presidential sounding board.***

Annual Review and Reporting to the Board

The Board chair should consider on an annual basis the internal and external crisis communication strategies that are in place. This review should include the president and the trustee who chairs the committee that includes communications. The chair may ask of the president the following:

1. Has an external crisis communications firm or consultant been identified? This service is often an insurance benefit. Or is this a skill that can be accomplished by the internal team?
2. Is an internal incident management team or task force in place?
3. Are regular tabletop exercises performed? Does the team incorporate feedback into improvements in the plan?

It may be helpful to present the work of an incident manager to the Board from time to time to reassure the Audit Committee, or possibly the full Board, that management is thinking about and planning for multiple contingencies.

Board Notifications

To ensure consistent expectations, the Board chair and president should discuss and agree, generally, upon what meets the threshold of Board notification. As important as it may be to the parties directly concerned, not every incident meets the standard of immediate Board notification. Most incidents can be aggregated into annual reports to the Board regarding the cases taken up by the Title IX office, the NCAA compliance office, the dean of students office, physical facilities, information and technology services, marketing/communications, etc. This reporting can be to the Audit or Executive Committee, depending on the Board's communication practices.

A chair should consider at these moments how Board minutes and materials are housed and distributed. A Board portal may contain all the materials from a given committee and Board members can be directed to those materials if they need information on the presentations from other committees. Again, communication practices vary and the chair should be mindful of the Board's expectations. Roles for internal and external communications should be discussed, including:

- Should the Board chair be the source of the communication to the Board, or is that task delegated to the president, with the support of the Board professional?
- Should the Board chair and Board be provided punctual updates on a serious, unfolding crisis, response, and resolution? How often and to what depth? In some cases this may include providing the Board and chair with agreed-upon talking points.

Crisis Response

It is important that the Board chair knows what, if anything, is expected of them when a crisis response plan is formulated. In a developing situation, the Board chair should be available to review the management response plan with the president, knowing that the resolution of incidents is, ultimately, under the management of the president.

Opportunities do exist for the Board chair to actively assist in a crisis situation. A Board chair should anticipate and redirect negative energy among Board members — whether it's inopportune questions, unwise public statements, internal conversations containing speculations, or second guessing — affording the president and institutional leaders the opportunity to focus on resolving the crisis.

The Board chair may share experiences, expertise, contacts, or other support with the president, when it would be helpful to the institution. Following an incident, the Board chair should be positioned to provide valuable insights during the after-incident review by the president and trustees. Finally, as the president's supervisor — and support — the Board chair should be effective in helping to maintain public trust in the president, administration, and institution.

Few Board chairs relish the work of crisis management, but a cool head and a steady hand can support the president and university leadership when they need it most.

Recommended Reading

Rosowsky, D., Gavazzi, S., & Gee, E. G. (2022, January/February). Leadership in times of crisis. *Association of Governing Boards of Universities and Colleges*. *30*(1). https://tinyurl.com/AGB-Leadership-in-Crisis

Chapter 9
Fostering Continuous Improvement of the Board

Board development takes place in many phases, beginning with the onboarding of new trustees. Chairs are responsible for seeing that incoming trustees feel welcomed, informed, and have the resources at their disposal to contribute in a meaningful manner. It is a common practice and helpful when welcoming busy trustees to provide a checklist-style outline of the onboarding schedule so a new trustee knows what orientation programming to expect and what other resources available to them as they begin their role on the Board.

Trustee Mentors

Linking new Board members with trustee mentors is a best practice of higher education governance. When selecting trustee mentors, the first resource a Board chair should consider are seasoned trustees who have several years of solid Board service, hold or have held leadership roles such as committee chair, and who have the respect of their colleagues. Next, chairs can be good matchmakers, considering personalities and backgrounds in making this match. By working with the Board professional, the chair can provide support so each new trustee feels welcomed, empowered, and responsible. Trusteeship is service and servant leadership.

Once a mentor for each new Trustee has been identified, invite the two to sit together at meetings and Board meals, as well as meet together outside of official activities, and encourage the mentor to transmit both knowledge and confidence to their mentee. The Board professional should provide a job description for the mentor, as well as a list of topics and resources to guide the mentee's learning. Be clear about what these mentor/mentee roles involve and their importance in shaping the future Board. Among today's new trustees are the future Board chair and Executive Committee members.

Orientation Programs

Each Board will have its own structures and customs for onboarding new trustees. Don't be afraid to innovate modalities during your term as chair. Some Boards ask new trustees to serve for two or three years on the Mission and Identity Committee so that they become deeply immersed in, and sense themselves responsible for, maintaining and supporting the institution at the core of its being. The AJCU offers a range of multi-day seminars for ongoing Board formation, which have the added advantage of cross-pollination among trustees from sister institutions.

In a word, onboarding new trustees in an integral fashion focuses equally on "why" as it does on "what." Jesuit higher education institutions are the products of four and a half centuries of distinctive development. With ever fewer Jesuits present at AJCU schools, ***the Board has an increasingly essential role in guaranteeing that the Jesuit charism endures, even and especially through change, growth, and adaptation.***

Board Development

Continuing trustees are also in need of regular opportunities to deepen their understanding of the institution's operations, challenges, opportunities, and mission. One way to assure growth is to rotate trustees regularly among committees, so that they continue to learn about the institution from a variety of vantage points. Online resources should also be refreshed and augmented to keep pace with developments in the higher education landscape and in the worldwide Society of Jesus. ***A Governance Committee of the Board should support the chair in the essential task of leading and managing the Board.***

Boards play an important role in the institution's life, and thus Board chairs are tasked with thinking about, and planning for, the Board's development. *Nemo dat quod non habet* — no one gives what they don't have. A Board can be highly effective only when it is attentive to its own learning curve, regularly evaluating its own performance, honest about its blind spots, committed to ongoing formation and continuous improvement, and constructively critical of its "way of proceeding," which is a very

Jesuit spiritual and organizational concept. This includes but goes beyond the self-evaluation and peer evaluation of individual trustees.

Some Boards commit themselves to an every-other-year retreat, whereby the regular business meeting is truncated to cover only essential, timely matters, and much time is devoted to deeper thinking, conversation, and introspection. A Board retreat is not the chance for the Board to solve a major problem at the school; that is the senior leadership's responsibility. ***A retreat should afford the Board, guided by the chair, to ask and answer the question: Are we doing our appointed job well and faithfully?***

An invited speaker with specific experience and wisdom concerning AJCU school governance may be a helpful catalyst. Be judicious, however, in inviting experts who do not know Jesuit higher education. Boards can profit from reading their articles, but often they are not prepared to animate self-examination, for they likely do not know, or do not know well, what makes a Jesuit institution unique.

Recommended Reading

Chaffee, E., Hultquist, K., Maxwell, D., & Wilson, D. (2024, December 11). *Leadership Succession and Support.* AGB. https://tinyurl.com/AGB-Leadership-Succession

O'Neil, C. (2025, March/April). How to Succeed at Succession Planning: Foundations of Consequence. *Trusteeship*, 33(2).

Chapter 10

Presidential Searches

Hiring and assisting the president is perhaps the most important responsibility of the Board and the Board chair. Leadership transitions often have powerful effects on higher education communities, eliciting responses ranging from grief to consolation, but almost always anxiety. Anxiety, in turn, is corrosive, particularly for relationships within a community. Minimizing anxiety to the extent possible while seeking and installing new leadership for the institution can be best accomplished with as much communication as possible. The slightest news about where things stand is always welcome.

While hiring a president is solely the responsibility of the Board, practices have emerged that both reduce institutional anxiety and help to ensure that the hiring process results in a leader who is broadly embraced at the outset. Those practices stem from the institution's shared governance environment that enfranchises its key constituencies — including but also going beyond the Board — in substantive roles across the search process.

It is worth noting that, because the school is a Jesuit work, the president is also entrusted with the mission of the institution and as such is called the "Director of the Work" in Jesuit parlance. Once selected by the Board, the new president will be missioned to that role by the Jesuit provincial superior of the region, usually at the first public ceremony or at the president's inauguration. To ensure that this process goes smoothly and that ***the Society's involvement adds value to the search and selection effort, the leadership of the Board and the provincial superior for the region should consult early in the search process*** (see Appendix B: *The Role of Jesuit Provincials in Presidential Transitions at AJCU Institutions*).

In a similar vein, the chair should consider reaching out to the chairs of other AJCU institutions — especially those that have recently completed a presidential search — to learn as much as possible from their experience. AJCU can assist in making these connections.

The Jesuit Conference of Canada and the United States (JCCU), representing the North American leadership of the Society of Jesus, and the AJCU, representing the regional Jesuit higher education network, have collaborated on a document titled "The Role of Jesuit Provincials in Presidential Transitions at AJCU Institutions" (see Appendix B). This resource provides guidance and recommendations for Boards on engaging the Society of Jesus when conducting leadership transitions. The Board and the Search Committee leadership should review this text and, as needed, discuss it among the trustees in anticipation of initiating a presidential search.

What follows is an outline of a search process, focusing on the most significant decisions the Board and the Search Committee must make along the way. The advice is general, so every Board must take into account their institution's precedents, governing documents, market positioning, and current political environment, adjusting these suggestions to suit the moment.

Timing and the Search Cycle

Today's presidential searches typically take about six to nine months. While there are exceptions, they normally occur in one of three time frames:

- The largest number of presidential searches begin in the fall, early in the academic year, and conclude in the late winter or spring. This is the period when aspiring presidents are most active in the marketplace and competition for the best candidates is the most robust.
- Second are searches that begin in the late spring, shortly before the end of the academic year. These searches recruit candidates over the summer, and they usually conclude before the end of the calendar year.
- Finally, there is a cycle early in the calendar year, commencing in early January and rushing to conclude before commencement. The new president will likely be leaving an administrative position that involves academic year commitments. The availability of candidates and the

desire for a summer start date for the new president can depend greatly on the candidate's availability and potential impact on the institution they are leaving.

Regardless of the timing of the search, presidential appointments typically begin in the summer, as close to July 1 as possible. Thus, the earlier in the cycle a president is appointed, the longer the transition into the new role — and often the new institution — will be. Usually, but not always, longer transitions are more seamless if they are planned and executed well.

Even before the search begins, the Board would be well advised to look objectively at how attractive the institution is in the marketplace. The best candidates will do extensive homework, starting with the institution's own materials and publications, and then moving on to accreditations, credit ratings, and other external measures of quality and health. Candidates will also look at the career of the outgoing president. They will want to know why the former president is leaving and will likely be curious about whether there are internal candidates.

The Market

Presidencies have become more difficult — and correspondingly briefer — over recent years. Virtually every key constituency, including Boards, faculty, alumni, students, and staff members, has become more demanding as institutional resources have grown scarcer. According to a 2023 study by the American

Council on Education, the average president has been on the job for fewer than six years. This means that transitions are happening more frequently, whether by personal choice or institutional necessity. As a result, 15% to 20% of all colleges and universities are looking for presidents in any given year.

Perhaps surprisingly, given the difficulty of the role and the relative lack of job security, people still wish to serve as presidents, whether or not they are well qualified. Thus, the marketplace is somewhat bifurcated — for example, presidential searches are still generating large candidate pools, but the pool of highly qualified and willing leaders is circumscribed. Generating a pool of 50-100 applicants is therefore not difficult but finding the most highly qualified dozen or so applicants within that pool has become much more challenging with each passing year. Chairs of Search Committees have often commented on the dearth of candidates who are well prepared to serve.

All of this refers primarily to traditional candidates, which is to say someone with an earned terminal degree who later was granted tenure and promotion, then served as a department chair, a dean, and/or a provost. Increasingly, non-traditional candidates are coming up through administrative careers such as student services, general counsel, or chief financial officer, often with a terminal degree or master's degree and commensurate professional experience. There may well be candidates from further afield: retired military, corporate officers, attorneys, etc. Such candidates usually have little to no idea how searches of this sort work and must be thoroughly oriented at the outset. They seldom voice the same constraints in terms of start dates, but can experience anxiety around confidentiality.

Executive Search Firms

Most presidential searches today are supported by professional executive search firms. AJCU has compiled a list of the firms that most often support such searches for member institutions. Other firms may also bring the right understanding of the environment and contemporary knowledge of the marketplace for a given situation. Search firms provide two primary services:

- Based on an understanding of the institution's needs and circumstances, they will actively recruit a robust candidate pool and will vet the most serious candidates in order to reduce risk.
- Based on an understanding of higher education generally and the institution specifically, they will lead a process that optimizes the chances for success in the search. They will offer direct support for each of the steps in the process.

Different firms — and even different consultants within those firms — have marginally different methodologies and experiences with various types of institutions (e.g., small and large institutions, liberal arts or research universities, different regions of the country, etc.). Fees and expenses vary somewhat as well, though typically firms charge one-third of the new president's first-year compensation, plus expenses. Institutions seeking support from search professionals are well advised to solicit multiple proposals and to vet the firms — and the individual consultants — to ensure not only the best business arrangements but also the best match with the institution's culture.

Any search firm worthy of a good reputation will not make decisions about candidates in the place of the Search Committee or Board, nor will it champion one candidate over another. All candidates should be highly qualified, and it is up to the Board and its Search Committee to choose the most apt leader.

Confidentiality

Before initiating any aspect of the search publicly, the Board must make a critical decision that will influence the entirety of the search: the level of confidentiality that will be afforded the candidates. Board members typically assume that the entirety of the search will be confidential, just as faculty members assume that the entirety will be completely transparent. If the Board chooses to include non-trustees on the Search Committee, they should join trustee members in signing non-disclosure agreements that bind the members in perpetuity to the Board's decisions around confidentiality.

There are, generally speaking, three kinds of searches in terms of confidentiality:

Completely confidential: The Board conducts the search without disclosing the identity of any of the candidates, until the hire is announced. In this scenario, few if any members of the institution's community beyond the Board meet with, help to recruit, or provide feedback on the final candidates. The chief advantage is that this methodology is familiar to most Board members. Candidates usually appreciate as much confidentiality as possible. The disadvantage is that campus communities, ever suspicious of the sources and use of power, may unfairly believe the new president has a hidden agenda or has received orders from the Board thus making a positive welcome almost impossible. A completely confidential search may lead some members of the larger community to "star chamber" accusations and may dog the new president's early days in office. Ironically, the best candidates don't always prefer this approach because it can undermine the credibility of the appointment.

Transparent: A completely transparent search, in which everything takes place "in the sunshine," with every aspect of the search — including the candidate pool — available for public scrutiny and comment, is extremely rare. Even public institutions required by statute to conduct their work in the sunshine usually find a way to allow candidates to discuss the job fully before being outed publicly. These days, the most customary way to conduct a transparent search is to ensure the institution's community that all final candidates will appear openly in the final round of interviews. This approach allows candidates to remain confidential until the odds of their being hired make the decision to go public more palatable. Its advantages are that everyone knows who the final candidates are, meaning that they know the outcome of the Search Committee's work and the options given to the Board. Everyone is given an opportunity to provide feedback to the Board to inform its decision. There are fewer mysteries or potential conspiracies, and the candidate of choice may then assume that the appointment benefits from the broadest possible buy-in from the institutional community.

The disadvantages are that, while there are many aspects of a search that are most efficiently handled in confidence — references and salary negotiations can both be compromised by the sunshine, for example — the best candidates, the ones in good jobs with the most options moving forward, will still be loath to participate. In fact, they often get cold feet just before going public, one of the worst possible times for a candidate to withdraw. It is a sellers' market for the very best candidates, and they know that they may well be compromised in their current job if their candidacy becomes widely known. This is especially true for sitting presidents. In today's world of social media, everything becomes widely known instantly.

Hybrid process: An AJCU-recommended hybrid process is built on an attempt to secure the confidentiality that will benefit the Search Committee's work and retain candidates until the final conclusion of the process. Here, the Search Committee deals with candidates in confidence through the process up to the moment that finalists are identified. Finalists visit the institution privately to meet with the Board and/or its leadership and with representatives of the key constituencies, singly or in smaller groups, who agree to maintain confidentiality and are then asked to provide feedback to the Board. The theory is that a small number of people can keep a secret better than many. Only the Board or Search Committee's chosen candidate will be known to the broader campus community. And, the candidate's home community is given the news only after securing an appointment by the Board. The biggest advantage here is that most traditional candidates will agree to this approach. They understand the dynamic between their privacy and the credibility of their appointment and will take the chance. Participants almost always live up to their oaths. The institutional community may rest assured that the final candidates were vetted by trusted members of their constituencies.

Some final considerations on hybrid or transparent approaches: Trust and willingness to delegate responsibility and authority can be hard to come by in academic communities. Non-traditional candidates may still find this too open for their liking. Not everyone lives up to their commitments though; more often than not, confidences are violated inadvertently, making this approach more of a gamble for candidates than a completely confidential search.

The Search Committee

As noted, hiring the president is the job of the Board, but over many years a usual and customary approach recognizing the importance of shared governance has emerged. In this approach, a Search Committee consisting of representatives of the institution's key constituencies is empaneled and charged with identifying a group of final candidates for the Board's consideration. Such committees usually are appointed by and report directly to the Board and work to its specific charge.

Among the Board's many considerations in creating the committee are the following:

Size: Generally speaking, the larger the committee, the more difficult the scheduling of meetings, and the more tempting it may be for individual members of the Search Committee to think of themselves as representatives of subgroups rather than of the school as a whole. Within reason, then, smaller committees tend to work more efficiently and effectively than larger ones. Is a large committee capable of carrying out its work efficiently, maintaining confidentiality, and, most important, able to meet all the finalists and semi-finalists in order to have discussions where all finalists have been equally vetted?

Representation: While most Boards will delegate the development of the candidate pool to a Search Committee, they nonetheless want that committee to reflect their priorities. The most effective way to ensure that is to impanel a committee with a majority of trustees. The next most critical constituency is the faculty, who will inevitably wish to have the predominant voice in the effort.

Finally, the Board must decide how many other constituencies must be represented and in what numbers. Among the constituencies under consideration are usually students, staff, alumni, the community (including the local Ordinary), and, of course, the Society of Jesus. In addition to vetting the candidate pool, the Search Committee is usually the first constituency candidates will encounter live during the search process, meaning that the committee must both represent the institution well and, importantly, be a font of information for candidates still engaged in their own decision-making process. The following hypothetical is an example of how a committee may be constructed:

- Trustees: Six, with one of them serving as chair. When possible, it is usually optimal to have on the committee whomever will chair the Board when the new president joins; if they can chair the committee, that is even better. It also frequently streamlines later aspects of the process if at least one of the trustees is a Jesuit and one or more are alumni.

- Faculty: Two, ideally from different disciplines and at different stages of their academic careers (e.g., a full professor, an associate professor, or an assistant professor). These faculty members can be selected by the Board or elected by their peers, depending upon precedent and the political environment.
- Student: One, ideally a leader from within the student body who is comfortable within the power dynamic of the group and, importantly, able to speak compellingly about the institution to the candidates. The very best candidates will often zero in on the student representative(s) with questions during preliminary interviews.
- Cabinet member: One, selected for both probity and institutional knowledge. Someone on the committee will need a fair amount of institutional data on hand to respond to candidates' questions; often a member of the president's leadership team is well suited to this role.
- Jesuit: One, typically a Jesuit trustee or the superior of the Jesuit community. In presidential searches, the U.S. provincials have recommended that a Jesuit be on the Search Committee. He will have a sense of who might be available should there be a real desire to have a Jesuit president. And, he will likely be among those to ask the mission questions that the Board underscores as important.

He may likely be working at another Jesuit university and have a sense of up-and-coming leaders.

With these categories accounted for, such a committee would total between 10 and 12, which is about as small as is usually possible. As the Board adds representatives from other constituencies, it should be sure that trustees constitute a majority. Thus, numbers tend to grow quickly to the detriment of the committee's efficiency and effectiveness.

Trustees are often curious or frustrated by such committees, not only because of their size, but sometimes by the provincialism that may emerge and the expectations that different constituencies bring to the work of the committee. There may be only a few trustees on the Search Committee who actually have a good sense of what a president actually does. Whichever of the three above-mentioned models is chosen, it is imperative that the trustees on the Search Committee are well versed in the Board's major priorities.

- *Charge:* The Search Committee should be charged with specific goals, responsibilities, and accountabilities. That charge and its acceptance by each member of the committee should be memorialized in writing. The charge should not be confidential; the institutional community should have access to the committee charge and to the eventual position description so that they, too, may hold both the Search Committee and the Board accountable for their performance in the process. The following are very often included in such a charge:

- Act in the best interests of the institution as a whole
- Conduct a search that solicits information, candidate names, and comments from as wide a circle as possible
- Fairly and without bias assess the candidates' abilities and experiences relative to the needs and the ethos of the institution, especially its Jesuit mission and Catholic values
- Present to the Board a list of finalists for full consideration, typically unranked, with a compendium of perceived assets and liabilities of the candidates
- Conduct the institution's and the Search Committee's business in strict adherence to the Board's decisions around confidentiality

Getting Started in the Search and Developing a Presidential Profile

A presidential search is an opportunity to take stock and hear from community members about their hopes, dreams, and fears. It can be revelatory for a Board to conduct a due diligence campaign in which they call upon the community to express their assessment of the institution's current circumstances, their hopes for change, their desires — both substantively and stylistically —

in their new leader, and their concerns over what stands in the way of success. When aggregated, the outcomes of such a study also make a compelling starting point for the new president.

Most institutions synthesize the findings of that due diligence into a position description — called by many names, but for our purposes a presidential profile — that may be used both to generate interest among potential candidates and as a rubric for the Search Committee and Board to use in evaluating candidates. The presidential profile is typically created by the search firm, after consultation with the Search Committee. While it is tempting to think of this document as a sort of sales brochure that hyperbolizes the institution's charms, it is critical that it also shed light on the challenges the new president will face. Too often, presidencies are compromised in their early days by critical information that was not shared in advance. Perhaps more importantly, the institution presumably needs someone with both the skills and drive to engage its problems and optimize its potential. The best way to find that person is to challenge him or her with the truth. ***Leaders want to lead and to accomplish things in the current context. The strongest candidates will embrace the institution's challenges and potential.***

Recruitment

Another use of the presidential profile is the generation of an advertisement for the job. While finding a president absolutely necessitates active and focused recruiting, most institutions do advertise the opportunity in various, typically trade, publications (for example, *The Chronicle of Higher Education*, *Inside Higher Ed*, etc.). The AJCU Job Bank is another customary posting site for Jesuit institutions. Such advertisements occasionally surface a strong candidate. More often, they lay the groundwork for a more ambitious and personal outreach to high-potential candidates. They can also serve as an opportunity for the institution to market itself within the higher education sector.

By far the most effective way to ensure a robust pool of candidates, however, is to recruit them personally.

Personal outreach is often initiated by the search consultant assigned to your case. Consultants and their firms who specialize in higher education leadership searches, and especially those who have supported searches at other Jesuit institutions, have a sense of who the rising candidates are. People who are actively seeking their next role like to be invited to apply for a position, for an expert has already considered them potentially a good fit. Once established, an ongoing dialogue with high-potential candidates increases the chances that they will apply. It also aids in the assessment of those candidates, given the more frequent and intimate level of exchange taking place.

The process of building an initial pool of qualified candidates is an opportunity to engage with the institutional community. Do Search Committee members know a dean or vice president elsewhere who may want to consider the position? Periodic updates on the process, often starting with the solicitation of nominations and referrals, engage the community and often also have the effect of reducing anxiety. Especially in a completely confidential search process, illuminating the steps and progress of the process can have a positive impact on the mood of the campus.

Assessment, Screening, and First Meetings

Generally, a formal application to be considered for a presidency consists of a cover letter and a curriculum vitae or resume. Some institutions require additional documentation focused on specific industry or institutional issues, such as leadership or diversity statements. Since initial candidate assessments are typically conducted based on those documents, the Search Committee will use the presidential profile as a rubric for narrowing the candidate pool to those meriting a preliminary interview.

Traditionally, presidential searches have involved two rounds of interviews, known as preliminary and final. With the growing ease of videoconferencing, some institutions have adopted a three-round approach: first a video interview, then a second interview being the more traditional in-person conversation, often referred to as the airport interview in reference to their most common venue. Usually the pool is narrowed with each resulting round. The pool of finalists emerges from these conversations, augmented by preliminary references and background checks.

Such an approach, then, might include something like 12 or so interviews in the first round, followed by around eight in the second, with a group of two to four finalists progressing to the final round. Thoughtful preparation is critical to this interviewing process. The first two rounds of interviews are typically fairly brief, perhaps an hour for round one and 90 minutes for round two. Using such a short period productively — and ensuring the fairness of the process — normally dictates the use of prepared questions that are asked of each candidate, with those questions becoming more specific to the circumstances of the institution in each round. It is absolutely vital for the Search Committee to treat the candidates fairly and hospitably, including by allowing them time to quiz the Search Committee on questions critical to their own decision-making process. Such interviews are two-way conversations; most candidates will not be hired, but it is imperative that they walk away with a positive experience of the process and an elevated and informed respect for the institution.

Finalist Interviews and Due Diligence

With the candidate pool reduced, typically, to two to four finalists, each interaction becomes more significant to the success of the effort. Information exchange becomes crucial. Finalists are usually provided with an extensive array of institutional data and often request even more. What one finalist requests, all should receive.

For their part, finalists will be expected to provide insight into their own backgrounds and previous performance, especially by granting permission for intensive referencing and by authorizing background checks. Candidates will provide a list of references; the search firm will typically also reach out to off-list references, people who know the candidate well but were not suggested by the candidate. Unlike searches for faculty members, referencing at the presidential level is generally accomplished by conducting live conversations with references rather than by soliciting letters. Extemporaneous conversations usually elicit more candid feedback. To reduce bias and assure legal compliance, such conversations are generally conducted around a standard set of questions and are memorialized in writing, the closer to verbatim the better.

AJCU institutions are led by someone with a keen sense of how the Catholic and Jesuit identity of the institution is studied, practiced, and enshrined in its mission statements and institutional policies. Individuals who are not Catholic will have a difficult time conveying the mission and representing the Catholic faith to internal and external audiences. During the interview process, both Catholic and non-Catholic candidates should be asked the same questions. For instance, "How do you see yourself contributing to — advancing, defending, and defining — how the Catholic faith grounds the institution's mission and identity?" The previously mentioned JCCU paper, "The Role of Jesuit Provincials in Presidential Transitions at AJCU Institutions," (see Appendix B) offers sample questions for assessing how well a candidate may represent and support the mission.

The provincial should be invited to comment on the dossiers of the small group of finalists, and to speak with them if he wishes to do so. He will share his opinions of the strengths and weaknesses with the Board chair and/or the Search Committee chair. This is more than a courtesy since the provincial will be missioning the individual as a "director of the work," that is, as the person responsible for maintaining the mission of the institution.

Deep background checks are usually outsourced to professional firms with the necessary resources and a comprehensive understanding of the laws governing such activity. Such checks generally include verification of degrees and previous employment, credit scores, criminal records, driver's license records, previous or current litigation, and sexual predator registries. Deep online searches for other information in the public domain are also frequently undertaken, but caution is advised given the abundance of misinformation on social media platforms.

Many institutions also request that their final candidates undergo leadership and/or psychometric assessments performed by industrial psychologists. These assessments are not tests; they do not result in a thumbs up or down outcome. They can, however, confirm or call into question the conclusions made by search firms, committees, and the Board during the more qualitative process of assessment undertaken by search firms, committees, and Boards.

Finalist interviews typically take place on or near campus, depending upon the level of confidentiality offered to the candidates. The Board as a whole or its representatives, and perhaps key constituents or their representatives, meet with each candidate in turn and then offer their assessments. Concurrently, those groups do their best to incentivize each candidate to accept the job if offered, thus a delicate balance is needed between challenging the candidates and providing them with exceptional hospitality. In no case, however, should any institutional representative convey to a candidate that he or she is their top choice.

Candidates are frequently invited to include their spouses or partners and even their children to accompany them on the visit. While the candidate is interviewing, the family is offered a tour of the campus and information about housing options, local schools, etc. In cases where the institution offers a presidential residence, a tour of the home should be included in the family's visit. A Jesuit candidate will be asked in advance whether he would like to stay in or visit the local Jesuit community during his visit.

Closing the Deal

While conducting the search, the Board should also be preparing for the moment that its new president is identified, secured, and introduced. Of particular importance is due diligence and discussion around compensation and perquisites. Federal regulations require, for example, that the Board be able to attest that the compensation it offers is commensurate with the marketplace, and substantial penalties, called intermediate sanctions, can be levied should the compensation offered be deemed excessive. As a result, some sort of analysis of the marketplace for similar appointments at similar institutions is recommended. The search firm will provide valuable information in this regard throughout the search process but are not always compensation consultants; your institution's human resources team should conduct its own process to ensure the viability of all data. Preliminary conversations about expectations around compensation and perquisites should be conducted with the candidates well in advance of their final interviews to ensure the likelihood of alignment and to eliminate candidates with unrealistic and unrealizable expectations.

In addition to salary and standard benefits, the following frequently come into play in the negotiations with leading candidates:

- Start date
- Relocation costs
- Incentive compensation, including both rewards and the methodology for setting and measuring progress toward goals
- Provision of academic rank and tenure (for traditional candidates), including details on compensation upon retreat to the faculty
- Deferred compensation
- Use of a presidential residence
- Use of an automobile
- Memberships in clubs or other organizations for fundraising or other promotional purposes
- Arrangements for any unexpected, involuntary separation, including the definition of "cause" and any severance arrangement

Note: A Jesuit candidate's salary will be sent to his community, as are the salaries of other Jesuits and religious working in the university due to their vow of poverty.

When the president has been selected and negotiations are complete, the institution has the opportunity to make news with its appointment. Institutional and local communities, in particular, will be anxiously awaiting the outcome of the effort. Assuming the selection has been confidential, ***it is critical that information about the new president be closely held until a public announcement is made.*** The first public announcement should be part of an overall communication plan that enables the institution to share the information strategically to its advantage. One example is providing advance word, by only a few hours, to selected institutional and local leaders, alumni, or donors, thus further cementing important institutional relationships. Calling the local Ordinary in advance of the announcement is often a welcome courtesy. If news of the appointment leaks out before the formal announcement, opportunities are lost for strategically bringing key constituents into the loop.

Transition

Particularly with traditional hires, there is typically a time gap between the announcement of the new president and that person's arrival on the campus. It is not unusual for that gap to be several months. The institution, therefore, has the opportunity to affect an organized and thoughtful transition for the new president and the outgoing leader. Boards are well advised to begin very early in the search process to anticipate how this honeymoon period — which ideally includes the first several months in office — may be organized in ways that are maximally productive while simultaneously smoothing the president's transition to their new role and/or community. Many institutions create formal, written plans for this important period that minimize both ambiguity and the inevitable competition for the new leader's attention. Needless to say, any such plans require the collaboration of the new president and their family, as well as accommodation for the institution from which they are departing.

These plans typically include celebrations of the outgoing leader's contributions and the arrival of the new leader. The latter may include a formal inauguration event, often a few months after the actual start date. This is an opportunity for the community to highlight its accomplishments publicly. It is also an important moment for the institution and the new leader to recommit themselves to their Jesuit, Catholic mission and values by including the local Catholic bishop, the Jesuit provincial superior, and the local Jesuit community as key participants. Civic leaders and outstanding alumni typically round out such celebrations, but the first focus should be on faculty, staff, and current students.

Off-cycle Searches and Interim Presidents

While the majority of presidential transitions are planned, often well in advance, it is increasingly the case that personal and institutional circumstances can lead to unplanned, even abrupt, departures. These often accompany challenges — or even crises — at the institution that add to the level of anxiety on campus and among trustees. If the outgoing president was beloved by some or most constituencies, that anxiety ratchets up even more.

All too often, such hurried circumstances lead the Board to forgo some of the critical recommended steps noted herein, particularly those around conducting due diligence or otherwise involving the campus community in the search process. Doing so is most often a bad decision, in part because the eventual hire is tarnished by accepting the position after a flawed process.

Boards should consider, among other factors, the academic calendar when judging the timing of such a search. Traditional candidates will still very often be bound by commitments until the end of the academic year. Also, it is very difficult to accomplish anything in higher education — particularly Catholic institutions — during the holiday period that typically runs from December 15 to January 15. Only under the direst of circumstances should a Board conduct an expedited search in the absence of substantive input and active participation from the institutional community.

Often, this means the appointment of an interim leader. While the nature of such an appointment is beyond the scope of this document, the Board is well advised that such an appointment will be closely scrutinized by both the campus community and the presidential marketplace. Whether accurate or not, assumptions will be made regarding the state of the institution and the intentions of the Board based on the background and personal qualities of the interim leader. As a result, active and clear communications regarding the intentions of the Board, the charge to and presumed term of the interim leader, and especially the plan for the search are particularly critical in this circumstance. Among the first questions to be asked will be the eligibility of the interim leader to be considered for the permanent post. Remembering the enhanced level of anxiety in an academic community, the Board may wish to anticipate this and make clear the response before being asked.

At a Glance: Keys to a Successful Presidential Search

While this section has explored the major aspects and milestones of a typical presidential search, there are a large number of possible variations. Institutional history, precedent, events leading to the transition, politics (both institutional and public), and any number of other factors may well require adjustments to the usual and customary presidential hiring process. Methodologies may vary, but the Board and its leadership would be wise to bear the following in mind in anticipation of a successful search effort:

- Plan thoughtfully and thoroughly while keeping both the process and the end result top of mind
- Involve the provincial superior and/or his representative in the planning to ensure alignment from the outset
- Anticipate the anxiety of the institutional community and seek to minimize it, particularly by making clear what

information will be shared and when, and what will be confidential

- Within that context, communicate actively and often during the conduct of the search to assure the community that progress is being made
- Proactively seek out the very best candidates — foregrounding their commitment to the Jesuit mission and Catholic identity of the institution
- Vet those candidates thoroughly while at the same time providing them with both the data and the hospitality that will be crucial to their decision-making
- Celebrate the outcome by putting the best of the institution on display
- Plan and execute a thoughtful transition

Recommended Resource

AJCU list of search firms, including RFPs and pricing strategies: https://ajcunet.edu/ajcu-search-firm/

Acknowledgements

A Guide for Board Chairs of Jesuit Colleges and Universities is a compilation of resources for the governance of Jesuit colleges and universities in North America and Belize. Deep appreciation is due to the many talented AJCU colleagues who authored portions of this volume. Their expertise is communicated on every page. We thank:

Letty Duenas, Loyola Marymount University

Jeff Feldhaus, Creighton University

Steven Frieder, Marquette University

Cecelia Gotham, Canisius University

Dorothy Marinucci, Fordham University

Mary Petersen, Seattle University

Desiree Rodriguez, Loyola University New Orleans

Chitchi Tabora, University of San Francisco

We are also grateful to the AJCU Governance Advisory Committee, whose members authored and reviewed chapters and served as an editorial board for the entire project. Abiding thanks are due to:

Dennis Barden, Barden Career Consulting

Joseph DeFeo, AJCU

Robert Farrell, University of Scranton

Rev. Michael Garanzini, S.J., AJCU

Will Johnson, Fairfield University

Bill Kaufman, Saint Louis University (Ret.)

Jacqueline Neesam, University of San Francisco

Stephanie Russell, AJCU

We thank Rev. Paul Fitzgerald, S.J. for his many contributions as an initial editor and Jacqueline Neesam for her project coordination. Talya Sanders ably copy edited the text. Cover art was generously provided by Holly Schapker, whose *Ad Sum* collection inspires this work.

A Guide for Board Chairs of Jesuit Colleges and Universities was underwritten by a grant from the Executives in Church-Related Higher Education Initiative of the Council of Independent Colleges. We are indebted to them for their generosity and confidence in this project.

Appendix A

Sample Conflict of Interest Policy Provisions

Examples: Purpose Statement

Example 1: The [Institution] governing board members, officers, and President's Cabinet members have fiduciary duties of obedience, care, and loyalty to [Institution], which require them to put [Institution]'s interests ahead of their personal interests and to act in the best interests of [Institution]. [Institution] recognizes that its leaders are engaged community members who have personal interests outside the scope of their responsibilities to [Institution]. When a transaction or activity involving a fiduciary's personal interests also involves the interests of [Institution], the fiduciary is considered to have dual interests. When dual interests give rise to actual or potential conflicts of interest, [Institution] must ensure its interests are protected. [Institution] has established this policy to provide for the timely disclosure of dual interests so [Institution] can protect its interests and avoid or appropriately manage any resulting conflicts of interest.

Example 2: [Institution]'s leaders have ongoing legal duties to act in [Institution]'s best interests. This policy is intended to help [Institution]'s leaders identify dual interest situations involving both their personal interests and the interests of [Institution], and to provide an oversight process for the disclosure, evaluation, and management of these dual interest situations, such that [Institution]'s actions on a matter involving dual interests will be perceived and treated as valid, binding, and appropriate, despite the perception or existence of a conflict of interest.

Example: Fiduciaries' Obligations

[Institution]'s fiduciaries strive to maintain the highest ethical standards whenever the interests of [Institution] are involved, both in perception and in fact. To that end, fiduciaries are expected to:

- avoid situations that may result in, or create the perception of, a fiduciary (a) using the fiduciary's relationship with [Institution] for personal gain; (b) losing independence or impartiality; or (c) adversely affecting [Institution]'s reputation;
- timely disclose any personal interests (including those involving their related parties) that may conflict with the interests of [Institution];
- fully cooperate in the evaluation, management, and oversight of all conflicts of interest identified by the Conflict Management Committee; and
- not vote on or otherwise seek to influence the decisions and actions of [Institution], its Board, committees, or other institutional decision makers on any subject giving rise to a conflict of interest with any personal interests (including those involving the fiduciary's related parties).

Consistent with applicable law, fiduciaries will not divert an [Institution] business opportunity for personal gain or the gain of others outside [Institution], use any confidential information acquired as a result of their service to [Institution] for any purpose other than the legitimate business interests of [Institution], or provide such information to any third party without proper authorization.

Example: Definition of Dual Interest

A dual interest is any of the following:

(a) an existing or potential ownership or investment interest in any entity with which [Institution] does business or is negotiating a business transaction or arrangement;

(b) an existing or potential compensation arrangement with [Institution] or with any entity or individual with which [Institution] does business or is negotiating a business transaction or arrangement (including direct and indirect remuneration as well as more than de minimis gifts or favors);

(c) an existing or potential governing board, leadership, or other position of similar influence in any entity with which [Institution] does business or is negotiating a business transaction or arrangement.

Example: Definition of Personal Interests and Underlying Definitions

Personal interests means the financial and other personal interests of the fiduciary and all of the fiduciary's related parties.

Related party means the fiduciary's family members and related organizations.

Family member means the fiduciary's spouse or life partner and the fiduciary's descendants, ancestors, siblings, and all of their respective spouses.

Related organization means any business, organization, or entity, other than [Institution], in which (a) the fiduciary serves as an officer, director, trustee, or partner; (b) the fiduciary or a family member has an ownership interest in excess of 5%; or (c) the fiduciary and/or the fiduciary's family members have a financial interest that, in view of all the circumstances, is substantial enough that it reasonably could affect the fiduciary's judgment with respect to the terms of any transaction to which the related organization is a party.

Examples: Definition of Conflict of Interest

Example 1 (includes de minimis exception with no dollar threshold): A conflict of interest is any dual interest that [Institution] determines, through the procedures in this policy, actually does or potentially could: (a) result in a more than de minimis economic benefit to a fiduciary or a fiduciary's related parties, or (b) prevent or inhibit, or reasonably be perceived to prevent or inhibit, a fiduciary's ability to exercise independent judgment in the best interests of [Institution], or to uphold the fiduciary's duty to put [Institution]'s interests ahead of the fiduciary's personal interests.

Example 2: A conflict of interest is any situation in which a fiduciary has dual loyalties to [Institution] and another party involved in a transaction or other arrangement with [Institution], or where the fiduciary's personal interests could influence or be perceived to influence the fiduciary's actions or decisions. Conflicts may arise without any impropriety by the fiduciary.

Example: De Minimis Exception as Part of Evaluation and Management Process

Transactions or arrangements in the following categories that involve dual interests or a conflict of interest are considered to be de minimis in nature and do not require advance review by the Committee. Management will have authority to determine whether to proceed with these transactions or arrangements, and approval by the Board or an authorized Board committee will not be required. However, management will annually disclose all such transactions and arrangements to the Committee:

- A single transaction or arrangement involving less than $25,000;
- Multiple transactions or arrangements with the same trustee or related party(ies) within a 12-month period that, in the aggregate, involve less than $25,000;
- Transactions or arrangements to provide [Institution] with routine, ordinary course services, so long as the provided services (a) remain within expense limits and other parameters established in advance by the Committee and (b) are performed under an established service-level agreement with [Institution] that has been approved by the Committee and involves an aggregate amount that does not exceed $250,000; or
- A benefit provided to a fiduciary or a fiduciary's related party solely because the fiduciary or related party is a member in a class of beneficiaries that [Institution] serves as part of its charitable activities (such as financial aid provided to students), so long as the benefit is available to all similarly situated members of the same class on the same terms or basis.

Transactions or arrangements that are not in one of these four categories and involve a conflict of interest cannot proceed without approval by the Board or an authorized Board committee, regardless of whether the matter otherwise would require Board or committee approval under applicable governing documents. For such transactions and arrangements, the Committee's determination and evaluation process will be included as an exhibit to the minutes or resolutions of the approving authority taking action on the matter.

Appendix B
The Role of Jesuit Provincials in Presidential Transitions at AJCU Institutions

Jesuit Conference of Canada and the United States – May 2025

In 2002, a surprisingly prescient document was jointly issued by the Association of Jesuit Colleges and Universities (AJCU) and the Jesuit Conference (now, the Jesuit Conference of Canada and the United States, or the JCCU). Called *The Role of the Society of Jesus in the Selection of a President for a U. S. Jesuit College or University*, the document in effect anticipated a shift in the relationship between the Society of Jesus and the institutions of higher education in sponsors in the U.S. (and Canada as well), a shift driven in part by the declining number of Jesuits — including, most especially, of Jesuits qualified to serve as higher education presidents. Since that document was issued in 2002, virtually all AJCU institutions have seen presidential transitions. Some have seen several. As a result, the network of Jesuit Catholic schools in the United States and Canada has acquired a great deal of experience in how to navigate these important transitions well, and not only bring in talented, capable senior executive leaders, but also strengthen in the process the important relationship between the institution's Board and the Society of Jesus, embodied in the local Provincial Superior. With the benefit of better than two decades of experience, now is a good time to update that 2002 document. This set of "considerations" is intended to do so. It is offered in the spirit of advancing our collaboration in the promotion of the Jesuit and Catholic Mission of these colleges and universities.

Over the last decade especially, we have seen a significant turnover in leadership at the top levels of our institutions as those leaders have become — overwhelmingly — lay women and men. At the same time, we have experienced a deep and sincere appreciation of the Jesuit and Catholic underpinnings of our schools on the part of newly chosen presidents. We have also been consoled by the seriousness and dedication Board leaders have exercised in their duty to select the most qualified candidates to lead their institutions, including candidates fully capable of appreciating and advancing their specifically Jesuit, Catholic character.

Our experience of the selection process and the care with which Board leadership has consulted widely has been, for the most part, quite positive. Chairs have given considerable time and thought to the process. Search Committees have worked diligently to find and propose candidates with impressive resumes and deep respect for the Jesuit outlook and tradition. We have been consoled as well by the way Board Chairs and Search Committees have solicited our input and the input of the AJCU. Our "considerations" here seek to pass on what we have found helpful for us in our effort to support you. We hope that you might find our reflections useful in your desires to keep the relationship between your institution and the Society healthy and vibrant.

We begin with the premise that since the beginning of the era of "separate incorporation" in the 1970s — when Boards of Trustees were expanded to include a majority of lay members and took on full responsibility for the fiduciary welfare of the institution as well as its leadership — the responsibility for selecting its chief executive officer and approving other senior officers has rightly fallen to the Board. At the same time (as the 2002 document notes), the Society of Jesus "as founding and continuing sponsor, is especially concerned to promote the Jesuit, Catholic character" of the institution's mission. How can we strengthen our collaborative role in the welfare of these important institutions going forward? We welcome your continuing reflection and dialogue on this. In the same spirit, we ask you to consider the following.

1. When the Board Chair anticipates that a president will be stepping down, the Chair should promptly inform the Provincial. The Provincial will be eager to know what the Chair sees as the challenges and opportunities faced by the University, what Trustees are hoping for in the next President, the timing of this transition, and any interim plans that have been made. The Provincial will likewise want to share his perceptions and offer whatever help he is

able. This is a good time as well for the Provincial to be briefed on the expected timeline of the search process and when he will have the opportunity to speak with finalists, should he desire to do so, and provide feedback to the Board and/or Search Chair.

2. As noted above, a significant issue will be the qualities hoped for in the new president. Are there specific areas of leadership the Board will especially be looking for in the new president? What background qualities will be important elements of the candidate's Curriculum Vitae? Are there internal candidates? Presidential transitions always contain the hope of strengthening the institution going forward; this is as true of the Jesuit and Catholic character of the institution as it is of any other quality. We offer below a list of possible questions for interviewing candidates relevant to this dimension of their responsibilities (see *Brief Checklist of Questions*, below).

3. These potential interview questions suggest an important point, namely that the concern of the Provincial that successful candidates represent well the University's Jesuit, Catholic identity should be owned by the Board and the search process itself as well. Several practices are helpful here. The presidential profile, or example, should foreground the institution's Jesuit Catholic identity and the importance of representing it well — indeed, of

championing it. We have also found the participation of at least one Jesuit on the Search Committee to be a useful way to encourage rich mission-specific conversations within the Committee. The specific search firm's understanding of and comfort with the institution's Jesuit, Catholic mission also cannot be underestimated.

4. Presidents of AJCU institutions are likewise key leaders within the Provinces where they are located. Each is a "Director of the Work," in Society of Jesus parlance. Thus, those who are selected are missioned by the Provincial in this duty and publicly tasked to shepherd the institution. Of course, championing and advancing the institution's identity as Jesuit and Catholic is part of this responsibility. A list of the kinds of duties typical of presidents of Jesuit universities is listed below. To be fair, the list is neither complete nor is it expected that a candidate must show competence in each of them. Some can be shared with a Chief Mission Officer, a Campus Ministry Director, the Superior of the Jesuit Community, or a pastoral figure familiar to the campus (see *Some Duties*, below).

5. Given these duties, it is important for the Board and the Search Committee (and the search firm) to know that the Society of Jesus almost always expects someone tasked with this responsibility to be a practicing Catholic. When one considers the kinds of responsibilities involved in

leading a Catholic University, our experience has been that deep "in the bones" familiarity with the Catholic Church (and with the Society of Jesus as well, ideally) is extremely important. This is not to say that there are never exceptions, but they have been rare.

6. The search process ought to include an opportunity for a discussion of the finalists and their backgrounds with the Provincial, as well as the opportunity for him to speak with them and provide feedback should he desire to do so (as noted above.) This is a good opportunity to discuss as well how the Board and Provincial will support whichever candidate is chosen. Because appropriate orientation and on-boarding plans are increasingly typical for these positions, the Provincial and Chair ought to discuss the dimensions of that plan which will address the institution's mission as Jesuit and Catholic. On the one hand, such on-boarding plans are *informational*; that is, they would contain such things as the institution's mission and vision statements, overviews of institutional mission formation efforts, recent reports from the Provincial Assistant's annual visits, a summary of the most recent Mission Priority Examen and subsequent efforts to enact its recommendations, and so on. Here, the Provincial's Assistant for Higher Education is an especially effective resource. As well, the plan should set expectations for

participation in the AJCU and the ACCU, for creating a relationship with the local Bishop or Archbishop, and for participation in the life of the Province. However — and importantly — a mission-specific on-boarding plan should likewise be *formational*. Ideally, it would encourage the new President to grow more spiritually astute as they develop as presidents, and there are a variety of ways in which this can happen. Interestingly, the current crop of lay presidents is asking for just this kind of opportunity — and observing as well that it is more apt to happen if it is a clear expectation of the Board.

7. As was mentioned above, the Provincial will formally mission the new President as the Director of the Work, normally within the Inauguration Ceremonies. Inaugurations are always joyous events, of course, and the insertion of a missioning ceremony into it underlines the specifically religious dimension of the institution's mission and the gift it is to its region and to the Church. Here, it is apt to observe that the particular circumstances of the institution and its relationship with the local Bishop or Archbishop may recommend the Provincial's involvement in the President's introduction to him.

It is a good idea for the Provincial, the Chair, and the newly selected President to meet as soon as possible, once the President has been named. It is often helpful to include the Provincial's

Assistant for Higher Education in these early sessions since he will be the usual point of contact for the Province and Provincial to the institution. All involved need to build a relationship of mutual trust and collaboration, especially since this particular presidential transition may be the only one to occur during their respective tenures.

Again, these considerations are offered out of our collective experience with the search and selection process. Our prayers are with you as you carry out your duties for the institution. And, if there is any way we can be of assistance, we welcome the opportunity.

Very Rev. Jeffrey Burwell, S.J., Provincial of Canada

Very Rev. Sean Carroll, S.J., Provincial of USA West

Very Rev. Thomas P. Greene, S.J., Provincial of USA Central South

Very Rev. Karl Kiser, S.J., Provincial of USA Midwest

Very Rev. Joseph M. O'Keefe, S.J., Provincial of USA East

Very Rev. Brian Paulson, S.J., President of JCCU

A Brief Checklist of Questions for Assessing Readiness for Mission Leadership

1. How does the Candidate express their interest and readiness for leading a Jesuit, Catholic institution? What elements of their background give confidence in their ability to do so?

2. Is the Candidate comfortable with handling the Church's positions on critical (and sometimes neuralgic) points? Does he or she show an agility, a depth of understanding and a level of comfort when speaking to issues without becoming too contentious?

3. Has the Candidate done his/her homework on the mission, history, and identity of the institution — as would be expected for any person seeking to lead a major organization?

4. Does the Candidate have a record of showing interest in such mission-specific questions and leadership opportunities? Are they eager to learn more?

Some Duties of the Director of the Work

1. The Director of the Work is tasked with ensuring that the Catholic and Jesuit identity is clearly articulated in official documents and publications of the institution and that

hiring, onboarding and orientation practices for all foreground it.

2. The Director speaks as needed on moral issues from a Catholic point of view.
3. The Director cultivates an ongoing working relationship with the local Bishop or Archbishop.
4. The Director engages in the challenge of guaranteeing academic freedom while at the same time articulating Church teaching.
5. The Director supports and promotes Catholic Social Thought and the Catholic Intellectual Tradition in the curriculum.
6. The Director assures the formation of Trustees regarding mission and identity.
7. The Director endorses the Mission Priority Examen and takes seriously its findings.
8. The Director demonstrates — by personal life, values, and behaviors — the school's Catholic character.
9. The Director participates in the Association of Jesuit Colleges and Universities and the Association of Catholic Colleges and Universities.

Made in the USA
Coppell, TX
03 September 2025

54264653R00085